MANHATTAN ON FILM

Walking Tours of
Hollywood's Fabled Front Lot

Chuck Katz

D1407678

Limelight Editions

First Limelight Edition November 1999

Copyright © 1999 by Charles D. Katz

All rights reserved under International and
Pan-American Copyright Conventions.
Published by Proscenium Publishers Inc., New York.

Manufactured in the United States of America.

Interior design by Mulberry Tree Press, Inc.
(MulberryTreePress.com)

Library of Congress Cataloging-in-Publication Data
Katz, Chuck.
   Manhattan on film : walking tours of Hollywood's
      fabled front lot / Chuck Katz.
   p.   cm.
   Includes index.
   ISBN 0-87910-283-7

   1. Motion picture locations--New York (State)--New
      York Guidebooks. 2. Manhattan (New York, N.Y.)
      Guidebooks. I. Title.

PN1995.67.N7K38 1999
791.43'627471--dc21   99-41345
                    CIP

Manhattan on Film

Walking Tours of Hollywood's Fabled Front Lot

*To Mom and Dad
for their never-wavering love and faith*

PREFACE

A few years ago, I was in Minneapolis on a business trip. When in a new and hopefully exciting city with a few hours to spare, I frequently scour the "What and Where" guides that most hotels provide, in order to find suggestions for the best ways to spend my free time. While looking through just such a publication in Minneapolis, I came across a short article written about the couple who had purchased the real-life first home of Mary Richards. For those who do not remember, Mary Richards was the fictional counterpart of Mary Tyler Moore, the beautiful, brainy and feisty television news producer in the long-running television series of the 1970s, "The Mary Tyler Moore Show."

Much to my surprise, the structure that housed Mary's first apartment on the show (not to be confused with the high-rise she moved into in the show's later years), populated with best-friend Rhoda and quirky Phyllis, a three- or four-story Victorian building with shuttered windows, actually existed. While the interiors were no doubt filmed on a sound stage in Hollywood (or Burbank), the building itself was a home to "real" people.

As I read the article about Mary's television "home," two things struck me. The first was that, contrary to my initial impression, not all television homes were located on those scenic streets in Hollywood that can only be accessed on the "back lot" tram tours provided by many of the major studios. In fact, houses on such "streets" are no doubt used over and over again, disguised, if necessary, to serve the needs of the new "residents." Of course, as anyone who has been on a tour of the back lots knows full well, such houses are nothing more than facades. As the tram makes a turn off the street, we see that there is nothing behind the front of the "house" save some two-by-fours and some nails.

But the other thing that struck me as I read about Mary's house was how much I would have liked to go and see the house for myself. To match up the television image with the real-life structure, I thought, would be quite exciting. This, of course, from the guy who spent three consecutive weekends hunting the regions of lower Manhattan for the *Ghostbusters* firehouse (it was worth the effort—see **Walking Tour 12: SoHo and TriBeCa**).

Unfortunately, my schedule in Minneapolis did not permit me the opportunity to visit Mary's house, but my interest was piqued. Upon my return to New York City, I began to think about all the locations in Manhattan that appear in films. Not just the obvious ones, like the Plaza Hotel or F.A.O. Schwarz (see **Walking Tour 1: 57th Street Shopper's Delight**) but more obscure ones, like the building where Oscar Madison (Walter Matthau) and Felix Unger (Jack Lemmon) lived in the movie *The Odd Couple* (see **Walking Tour 3: The (Upper) Upper West Side**).

Over the years, Manhattan has served as the location of choice for hundreds of movies. And while most of the action in some movies takes place almost entirely within the city (e.g., *Sea of Love, Ghostbusters, One Fine Day*), others find a reason to stop in for a quick visit (e.g., *Moonstruck, Lost in America*). I began to watch movies set in New York City with a different slant, to see if I could identify the street, building or other location that served as the backdrop for a particular scene.

What began as a curiosity rose to the level of full-grown obsession. The result of that obsession?

You are currently holding it in your hands. Wherever possible, I have limited the book to locations that are still in existence. In a fast-paced, ever-changing social and business scene, where restaurants close and reopen almost overnight, this has not been an easy task. Some locations (e.g., The Empire State Building) are presumably here to stay. Others (e.g., O'Neal's Balloon, Columbus Avenue and 63rd Street) have played their part in New York's movie history and moved on. In some cases, I have indicated where a now vanished movie landmark had been. I apologize in advance for those locations that exist as this book goes to press (September, 1999) but are destined not to be there even a short time later.

Each Walking Tour is set up by neighborhood, and is intended to take no more than two hours, unless otherwise indicated at the beginning of the Walking Tour. Each is obviously best enjoyed on foot. How you get to the starting point is a matter of individual choice, although I have done my best to start each Walking Tour as close as possible to a bus and/or subway stop and have identified the means of mass transit that can get you to that stop. For purposes of these directions, it has been assumed that the TourWalker is starting out from a point within Manhattan. Directions are given from points north, south, east and west of each Walking Tour's starting point. Buses should be exited at the nearest stop to the one indicated.

The focus of the Walking Tours is the exterior of the building or other location. Thus, when I point out a building and indicate that it is where a particular family lived (e.g., the McCoys in *Bonfire of the Vanities*), I do not mean to suggest, since I do not in fact know, that any of the movie's interior scenes were filmed there.

These Walking Tours do not require entrance to a building, but some of the buildings are open to the public. Whether to enter a building or not is entirely up to the TourWalker. But please be on best behavior. TourWalkers have a reputation to uphold.

Clearly, each Walking Tour's attractions need not be viewed in the order provided. Each such route is offered merely as a suggestion, though it has been designed to give the TourWalker the shortest distance between one location and the next.

I employed no magic in determining which locations were used in a film. Most were found by watching the film and doing a little research. For example, I found Location 24 of **Walking Tour 4: The Upper East Side** by noting some stores that appeared in the background of the scene (the movie was *Ransom*) and locating those stores. Once I did that, I knew the movie site was across the street. A few locations were easier for me to find because I've lived in Manhattan a long time and I know the city and its neighborhoods reasonably well; but almost all locations could be found by anyone willing to take the time and make the effort.

It is strongly suggested that all Walking Tours be followed during daylight hours. The main reason is that it's easier to see and enjoy the locations in detail during the day. That aside, although none of the Walking Tours will necessarily take the TourWalker into unsafe areas, anyone walking around with his or her nose in a tourbook after dark not only will have some difficulty reading, but may become an invitation for unsavory characters to emerge from the shadows.

As I often refer to a location in terms of direction (e.g., northeast corner of a particular intersection, or west side of a particular avenue), it will be necessary for the TourWalker to understand these directional references. The city's "compass" is easier to grasp than you might imagine. For example, coming uptown and standing at the intersection of Second Avenue and 85th Street, you will find that 86th Street is ahead of you, north of 85th (while 84th is behind you and south) and

First Avenue is to your right, east of Second (while Third Avenue is to your left, west). If you are unsure of the directionals, consult the map at the start of each Walking Tour or simply ask one of the friendly New Yorkers walking by. They will be only too happy to help.

According to that "What and Where" guide in Minneapolis, the story goes that the people who purchased the Victorian house had not known it was the exterior for the television show and, growing weary of the continuous procession of tour buses pulling up in front of the house at all hours of the day and night, threw in the towel and moved to a less well-known location. Luckily, because Manhattan has hundreds of movie and television locations, not just one, the fate of the owners of Mary Richards' house should not be repeated here and for TourWalkers who like the small tube as well as the big screen, I have also included a few locations from some of the more popular television shows of recent years that have utilized Manhattan for their backdrops.

Finally, I sincerely hope that the TourWalkers enjoy taking these tours as much as I enjoyed putting them together.

Chuck Katz
September, 1999

ACKNOWLEDGMENTS

I would like to express my gratitude to the following: my loving family, particularly Mom, Dad, Jeff, Jim, David, Amy, Jacquie and Lyndsay, for their confidence and support as I embarked on this new career; my friends, for standing by me, helping me to believe in myself and treating me to the occasional meal; and Mel Zerman, for taking a chance and sharing my vision.

Contents

MANHATTAN ON FILM

Walking Tours of
Hollywood's Fabled Front Lot

Walking Tour 1
57TH STREET SHOPPER'S DELIGHT

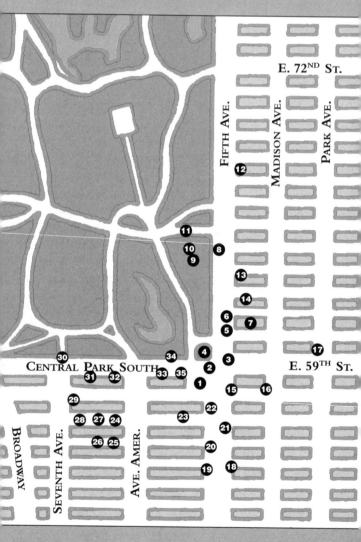

Walking Tour 1

57TH STREET SHOPPER'S DELIGHT

$\int$ome of the most expensive real estate in the world can be found within a short walk of the densely-peopled intersection of Fifth Avenue and 57th Street. Not only that, but go a short distance in either direction and you will find that this part of Manhattan has a rich and storied Hollywood history, with building after building and store after store finding a way into the movies.

Walking Tour 1: 57th Street Shopper's Delight begins at the southeast corner of Central Park, at the intersection of 59th Street (Central Park South) and Fifth Avenue. If you choose to get to the starting point by public transportation, you may use any of the following subway or bus lines (although the following list is by no means exhaustive):

FROM THE NORTH
SUBWAYS
- **4, 5** or **6** southbound to 59th Street. Walk west on 59th to Fifth Avenue.
BUSES
- **M1, M2, M3** or **M4** southbound on Fifth Avenue to 59th Street.

FROM THE SOUTH
SUBWAYS
- **4, 5** or **6** northbound to 59th Street. Walk west on 59th to Fifth Avenue.

- **E** or **F** northbound to Fifth Avenue and 53rd Street. Walk north on Fifth to 59th Street.
- **N** or **R** northbound to 59th Street, just west of Fifth Avenue. Walk east on 59th to Fifth Avenue.

BUSES

- **M1, M2, M3** or **M4** northbound on Madison Avenue to 59th Street. Walk west on 59th to Fifth Avenue.
- **M5, M6** or **M7** northbound on Avenue of the Americas to 59th Street. Walk east on 59th to Fifth Avenue.

FROM THE EAST
BUSES

- **M31** southbound on York Avenue to 57th Street, then westbound on 57th to Fifth Avenue. Walk north on Fifth to 59th Street.
- **M57** westbound on 57th Street to Fifth Avenue. Walk north on Fifth to 59th Street.

FROM THE WEST
SUBWAYS

- **1, 9, B** or **C** southbound to 59th Street/Columbus Circle. Walk east on 59th to Fifth Avenue.

BUSES

- **M5** southbound on Riverside Drive, then Broadway, then eastbound on 59th Street to Fifth Avenue.
- **M7** southbound on Columbus Avenue, then Broadway, then eastbound on 59th Street to Seventh Avenue. Walk east on 59th to Fifth Avenue.
- **M104** southbound on Broadway to Columbus Circle. Walk east on 59th to Fifth Avenue.

If you are not already there, cross to the west side of Fifth Avenue and get an unobscured view of the Plaza Hotel.

**1. 59th Street, west of Fifth Avenue. The
Plaza Hotel.** The name has become synonymous with class and elegance. Situated on one of
the busiest corners in all of Manhattan, the Plaza
Hotel stands grandly before the southeast entrance to Central Park.

One of those places that finds its way into film
after film, the Plaza is where, having boarded the
wrong plane and found himself in New York,
alone, at Christmas, Kevin McAllister (Macaulay
Culkin) checked in, under the suspicious eye of
the hotel's concierge (Tim Curry), in *Home Alone
2: Lost in New York*. In front, he ran into some old
friends.

It is also where Mick Dundee (Paul Hogan)
stayed and charmed the hotel staff, in *"Crocodile"
Dundee,* and where Monty Brewster (Richard
Pryor) resided during the 30-day period in
which he had to spend $30,000,000, in *Brewster's
Millions*.

In addition, the Daytime Emmy Awards were
held here in the movie *Soapdish*, starring Sally
Field, Kevin Kline and Elisabeth Shue, among
others.

In a fancy restaurant within the Plaza, smitten
and besotted Arthur Bach (Dudley Moore) dined
with a hooker he had picked up on the streets, in

23

Arthur. He expressed surprise (to the consternation of the other diners) when he learned that his "date" was a hooker. He had simply thought he was doing really well with her.

In an earlier time, newlyweds Paul (Robert Redford) and Corie (Jane Fonda) spent their very amorous honeymoon in the hotel, in *Barefoot in the Park*.

After his release from prison, Frank White (Christopher Walken) used the Plaza as the base of operations as he attempted to reclaim his crown as King of New York, in *King of New York*.

Just out front, near the fountain, F.B.I. Agent Mike Downey (Matthew Modine) trailed mob widow Angela Demarco (Michelle Pfeiffer) as she searched for a job. While she was inside a building across the street (the General Motors Building), Agent Downey passed the time singing with a group of street minstrels, in *Married to the Mob*.

———·•·———

Head north and cross 59th Street (Central Park South) to the north side of the street.

2. Central Park South and Fifth Avenue. Intersection. While waiting for the light to change at this intersection, Kevin McAllister, held captive by long-time nemeses Marv (Daniel Stern) and Harry (Joe Pesci), in *Home Alone 2: Lost in New York*, cleverly orchestrated his escape. He pinched the butt of an attractive woman standing in front of them. She turned around and clobbered the two goons, assuming one of them had the roaming fingers. Euphoric, Kevin ran off into the relative safety of Central Park.

———·•·———

Now, look across Fifth Avenue.

3. 781 Fifth Avenue. Sherry Netherland Hotel. Another grand hotel in the old tradition, the Sherry Netherland was home to Miss Zoe Montez (Heather McComb), where she essentially lived alone, with her butler, because her parents were always jetting around the world, in Francis Ford Coppola's "Life Without Zoe" segment of *New York Stories*.

The small block you are on is known as Grand Army Plaza. Continue north a few steps along Fifth Avenue. Note the statue on the left.

4. Fifth Avenue between 59th and 60th Streets. Statue. After his life took a tragic turn, once-hot radio talk show host Jack Lukas (Jeff Bridges) sat at the base of this statue, trying to drink away his sorrows. When that didn't work, he considered ending it all, until he met the mysterious and troubled Perry (Robin Williams). The rest is the stuff of fantasy, in *The Fisher King*.

Years earlier, before the statue was even there, journalist Phil Green (Gregory Peck), a new arrival to New York, walked through this plaza with his son Tom (a young Dean Stockwell) and sat on a bench near Fifth Avenue, talking about a great many things, in *Gentleman's Agreement*.

Continue north along Fifth Avenue, until you are halfway between 60th and 61st Streets. Look across Fifth Avenue.

5. Fifth Avenue (between 60th and 61st Streets). The Pierre Hotel. Another well-known symbol of luxury and excellence, this hotel was renamed "The Bradbury" for the movie *For Love or Money*. It is where concierge Doug Ireland (Michael J. Fox) worked to get anything and everything for his well-tipping guests.

In another film where the hotel was called "The Bradbury," finance whiz Laurel (Whoopi Goldberg) met Mr. Fallon (Eli Wallach) to try and convince him to do business with her and her fictional partner, Robert S. Cutty, in *The Associate*.

Walk north the short distance to 61st Street. Again, look across Fifth Avenue.

6. Fifth Avenue and 61st Street. Cafe Pierre. Soon after receiving unwanted custody of a baby, J.C. Wyatt (Diane Keaton) attended a lunch meeting at Cafe Pierre, where, with limited success, she tried to leave the baby with the coat check girl, in *Baby Boom*.

Look up at the tower above the Pierre Hotel, just across Fifth Avenue from you.

7. 2 East 61st Street. Pierre Hotel Tower. As his 65th birthday approached, wealthy communications mogul William Parrish (Anthony Hopkins) received an unwelcome visit during a family dinner from a mysterious stranger (Brad Pitt) in his New York City apartment. In *Meet Joe Black*, that luxurious apartment was high atop this building.

Continue north on Fifth Avenue until you reach the entrance to the Central Park Zoo and the Central Park Arsenal (at 64th Street).

8. Fifth Avenue and 64th Street. After finally agreeing to adopt a baby with his wife Amanda (Helena Bonham Carter), Lenny (Woody Allen) became the model father, in *Mighty Aphrodite*. In

the first scene shown with the baby, Amanda and Lenny, with carriage in tow, walked north along Fifth, in front of this entranceway.

If you wish to skip the following short detour through the Central Park Zoo, head north on Fifth Avenue, and skip to Location 12. If you choose to descend the stairs, continue until you are facing the Administration Building, known as the Arsenal. Turn toward the right and follow the path around at the end of the Arsenal.

9. Central Park Zoo. Babe (Dustin Hoffman) finally convinced the mysterious Elsa (Marthe Keller) to go out with him, in *Marathon Man*. For their first date, they went to the Central Park Zoo.

During a late-night transformation into a ferocious canine, book editor Will Randall (Jack Nicholson) stalked the caged animals in this zoo, sending them into a wild frenzy. When two police officers tried to apprehend him—one of them was played by David Schwimmer (Ross, on the television comedy "Friends")—Will leapt onto a nearby rock and disappeared into Central Park, in *Wolf*.

Walk up to the fence in front of you.

10. Central Park Zoo. Outdoor Patio. Unhappy at home, but knowing that meeting another man in the middle of the day was a big step, Alice (Mia Farrow) stood on the patio, trying to decide what to do, in Woody Allen's *Alice*. While she waited outside, the man with whom she was to have her rendezvous, Joe (Joe Mantegna), stood nervously inside one of the buildings, waiting for her.

Turn right and walk toward the archway known as the Delacorte Clock, with the sculpture of the elephant and bear on top.

11. Central Park Zoo. Delacorte Clock.
Later on in *Marathon Man*, Babe walked Mr. Szell
(Sir Laurence Olivier) at gunpoint under this
arch.

———— ·•·—— ————

Continue under the archway and follow the
path toward the next overpass. Go through the
overpass and stay to the right. There should be a
long line of benches on your right. Follow the
curve of the right-most path. You will exit the
park at 67th Street and Fifth Avenue. Turn left on
Fifth Avenue and head north until you are between 67th and 68th Streets.

**12. 860 Fifth Avenue (between 67th and 68th
Streets)**. Flanders Kittredge (Donald Sutherland)
and his wife Ouise (Stockard Channing) lived in
lavish style in this building until the tranquility
and sterility of their lives was ultimately shattered
by a mysterious visitor, Paul (Will Smith), in *Six
Degrees of Separation*.

———— ·•·—— ————

Cross Fifth Avenue at 67th Street and head
south (in the direction of traffic) until you get to
63rd Street. Cross 63rd and turn left, stopping at
the entrance to the building on the corner.

13. 817 Fifth Avenue (at 63rd Street). What
would a whirlwind New York City weekend be
without a little rendezvous with a member of the
fairer sex? If you are Lieutenant Colonel Frank
Slade (Al Pacino) and you have very little to look
forward to in your life, such a pick-me-up might
be just the thing you need. In *Scent of a Woman*,
while his "chaperone" Charlie (Chris O'Donnell)
waited in a car at the curb, Frank visited a woman
in this building.

———— ·•·—— ————

Return to Fifth and turn left. Walk south one
block to 62nd Street. Cross 62nd and turn left.
Walk the short distance to 8 East 62nd Street.

14. 8 East 62nd Street. Having just been promoted to detective, New York City policeman Michael Keegan (Tom Berenger) received his first assignment: protecting wealthy socialite Claire Gregory (Mimi Rogers), who witnessed a murder, in *Someone to Watch Over Me*. Miss Gregory lived in this building, where Detective Keegan learned that more was at stake than just a murder conviction or the safety of the witness: his marriage.

Return to Fifth Avenue and turn left. Walk south until you get to F.A.O. Schwarz (across from the Plaza Hotel).

15. Fifth Avenue and 58th Street. F.A.O. Schwarz. A tourist attraction in its own right, this fabled and always crowded toy store is where Mr. MacMillan (Robert Loggia) went every Saturday to get the pulse of the people, and where he ran into Josh Baskin (Tom Hanks), in *Big*. It is where the two of them performed a memorable duet of "Heart and Soul" and "Chopsticks" on the "foot piano."

A few years after they became friends, Lenny, with his adopted son Max, ran into Linda Ash (Mira Sorvino) with her daughter, inside the store, in *Mighty Aphrodite*. Neither Lenny nor

Linda knew the full extent to which their lives were intertwined.

If you choose to enter the store, I cannot be responsible for how much money you end up spending while inside, but it is certainly a great temptation. You might end up like hard-working concierge Doug Ireland who entered the store empty-handed and emerged with a large stuffed giraffe, which he then drove around, neck out of the sun roof in his hotel's limousine, in *For Love or Money*.

If you enter the store, you may exit on Madison Avenue. If you do not, walk east on 58th Street, alongside the store, until you get to Madison Avenue. Turn left.

16. Madison Avenue and 58th Street. F.A.O. Schwarz. The movie is *Baby Boom*, and "Tiger Lady" J.C. Wyatt was doing her best to accommodate the unexpected arrival of a baby in her life. After a big shopping spree, J.C. was seen exiting F.A.O. Schwarz on the Madison Avenue side, and piling her packages into a waiting cab at the corner.

Head north on Madison for one block, until you reach the north side of 59th Street. Turn right on 59th and walk one block east, until you get to Park Avenue.

17. 502 Park Avenue (at 59th Street). Christie's. Until the Spring of 1999, this building was the home of the famous auction house, where Annie (Diane Keaton) auctioned off all of the belongings of Elise (Goldie Hawn) and Bill (Victor Garber), in *The First Wives Club*. As part of her divorce, Elise had sold Annie all of the belongings for $1.

Head south on Park Avenue until you reach

57th Street. Turn right on 57th and walk west. Turn left on Madison Avenue and head south for two blocks. Turn right on 55th Street and head west until you are standing across from the St. Regis Hotel.

18. 2 East 55th Street. The St. Regis Hotel. Another beautiful hotel in an area rich with them, the St. Regis Hotel was the site of the first secret rendezvous between Elliot (Michael Caine) and his wife's sister Lee (Barbara Hershey), in Woody Allen's *Hannah and Her Sisters*.

In front of this hotel, cab driver Travis Bickle (Robert DeNiro), after he and the city had recovered from his wild shooting spree (an effort to rid the streets of scum), picked up the beautiful Betsy (Cybill Shepherd), at the end of *Taxi Driver*.

Within the St. Regis Hotel, at the famed King Cole bar, spurned first wife Elise Eliot tried to drown her sorrows with the help of a sympathetic bartender, in *The First Wives Club*. Elise was bemoaning the fact that she had been offered the role of a mother in a play, confirming her fears that she was, indeed, getting older.

———•◆•———

Walk the short distance west to Fifth Avenue. Before heading north, look diagonally across the street, to another beautiful hotel, this one, The Peninsula.

19. 700 Fifth Avenue (at 55th Street). The Peninsula Hotel. In the typical disaster movie, the audience is introduced to the cast of characters one-by-one or two-by-two, prior to the onset of the disaster. In *Daylight*, taxi-driver Kit (Sylvester Stallone) picked up two nasty passengers in front of this hotel, and had the harrowing task of driving them through the ill-fated Holland Tunnel. To find out whether they make it, you'll have to see the movie.

Renamed "The Barclay Hotel," this is where

self-styled lothario Joe Buck (Jon Voight) went to service one of New York's supposedly "lonely" women, in *Midnight Cowboy*. Apparently, the staff of the Barclay Hotel didn't share Joe's sense of the importance of his task, because they tossed Joe out on his rear end, while his friend and manager Ratso Rizzo (Dustin Hoffman) waited in the shadows.

In addition, radical attorney Edward J. Dodd (James Woods) was invited to come here to meet with Manhattan District Attorney Robert Reynard (Kurtwood Smith) to discuss a case that both men were working on, in *True Believer*.

Turn right on Fifth and head north. Stop when you are across from Harry Winston Jewelers, at 718 Fifth Avenue and 56th Street.

20. 718 Fifth Avenue. Harry Winston Jewelers. Holden (Edward Norton) wanted to buy his girlfriend Skyler (Drew Barrymore) an engagement ring and brought along his girlfriend's sister D.J. (Natasha Lyonne) for help. As with everything else in the Woody Allen film *Everyone Says I Love You*, their shopping spree turned into a full-scale musical number, right here in this store.

Continue north a short distance until you are in front of Tiffany's, at 727 Fifth Avenue and 57th Street.

21. 727 Fifth Avenue. Tiffany's. The name alone should give it away. Mysterious, beautiful "socialite" Holly Golightly (Audrey Hepburn), eating her breakfast pastry and drinking her coffee, stood in front of the store and admired the window displays at the beginning of *Breakfast at Tiffany's*. Later on, she got to wander inside with her suitor and neighbor, Paul (George Peppard).

After first arriving in New York, and filled with wonder and excitement, Joe Buck noticed a man lying on the pavement in front of this store, in *Midnight Cowboy*. What seemed to trouble him more than anything was the seeming callousness of the passersby, who barely looked at the figure on the ground. TourWalkers will learn that New Yorkers are not like that.

Cross 57th Street and then turn left, crossing Fifth Avenue. Walk the very short distance north on Fifth Avenue until you reach Bergdorf-Goodman.

22. 754 Fifth Avenue. Bergdorf-Goodman. Although Mr. Hobson (Sir John Gielgud) remarked that one would ordinarily have to go to a bowling alley to meet someone of similar stature, millionaire lush Arthur Bach did just fine on his own outside this

store, where he watched, with admiration, the

sticky fingers and quick wit of Linda (Liza Minnelli), in *Arthur*.

Return to 57th Street and turn right. Head west on 57th until you are standing in front of 9 West 57th. [Note: the large red "9" makes the address unmistakable.]

23. 9 West 57th Street. After quitting their high-stress lives and dropping out of society in an effort to "find themselves," David (Albert Brooks) and wife Linda (Julie Hagerty) instead found that chucking it all was not as easy as they thought it would be, in *Lost in America*. Finally realizing that withdrawing wasn't the answer, they left their current jobs in Arizona (he was a school crossing guard and she sold hot dogs at a fast food stand), drove their recreational vehicle all the way to New York City, and pulled up at the curb in front of this building. They may have gotten "lost" in America, but they "found" themselves in New York. Many people do.

For friends of "Friends", the hit television comedy series, it may be interesting to know that Chandler (Matthew Perry) worked in data processing in this building.

Continue walking west until you reach the Avenue of the Americas. Cross the Avenue to the west side of the street, cross 57th Street to the south side of the street, and walk west until you are in front of the Atrium to the Parker-Meridien Hotel.

24. 118 West 57th Street. Meridien Hotel. Assistant District Attorney Tom Logan (Robert Redford) was roped into giving the keynote address before the Manhattan Legal Society, which met here, in *Legal Eagles*.

For a very short detour, walk through the hotel lobby and out to 56th Street. As you emerge on

56th Street, walk to the curb and note the Air France storefront office directly across the street.

25. 120 West 56th Street. Air France. Finally deciding she had had enough, and more than a little smitten with Joe (Woody Allen), the beautiful Von (Julia Roberts) bought an airline ticket to Paris, and then emerged from this office, in *Everyone Says I Love You*.

Turn around and note the entrance to the hotel you just came through.

26. Parker-Meridien Hotel. 56th Street Entrance. Belinda (Shelley Long) developed feelings for Chuck (Henry Winkler), who, thanks to the cleverness of Billy (Michael Keaton), had become a pimp of sorts for Belinda and her cohorts, in *Night Shift*[1]. Sitting in a car with Billy in front of this entrance, with a customer waiting upstairs, Belinda had a decision to make and, surprisingly, Billy came through with some solid advice.

Go through the hotel's atrium and reemerge on 57th Street. Turn left and walk west on 57th until you reach 146 West 57th Street. It is the tall, black, triangular-shaped building between Sixth and Seventh Avenues. Look up.

27. 146 West 57th Street. Metropolitan Tower. This imposing structure was home to Jack Lukas, in *The Fisher King*, before a tragic shooting spree, possibly suggested by him to a caller to his radio talk show, turned his life upside down.

There are two ways to get to Carnegie Hall. One, as the old saying goes, is to practice. The

---

[1] Incidentally, fans of Kevin Costner may want to watch the movie again just to catch a glimpse of the star at a fraternity party held at the morgue (which is not located in this hotel).

other, and much quicker way, is to walk west a very short distance.

28. 154 West 57th Street. Carnegie Hall. Well-known symphony conductor Claude Eastman (Dudley Moore) suspected that his much younger and very beautiful wife Daniella (Nastassja Kinski) was cheating on him. To make things worse, Claude thought the affair was with fellow musician Max Stein (Armand Assante), with whom Claude was currently working, here, in *Unfaithfully Yours*.

Some TourWalkers may remember a 1947 movie called *Carnegie Hall*. It featured such classical music artists as Artur Rubinstein, Leopold Stokowski, Jascha Heifetz, Ezio Pinza, and the New York Philharmonic, and you are looking at where much of it was filmed.

Continue walking west to Seventh Avenue. Cross Seventh, then turn right, cross 57th and walk north up Seventh (against the traffic) until you reach the far corner of 58th Street. Turn and look diagonally across Seventh Avenue, to the beautiful structure on the southeast corner.

29. Seventh Avenue and 58th Street. Caterers Holly (Dianne Wiest) and April (Carrie Fisher) met David (Sam Waterston, in an unbilled role), an attractive and interesting architect, at a party they were catering, in *Hannah and Her Sisters*. After the party, David took the two women on a tour of what he considered to be some of Manhattan's more interesting architectural structures. This building, housing the restaurant Petrossian at ground level, was one of the buildings on that tour.

Go north on Seventh Avenue until you reach Central Park South (59th Street).

30. Central Park South and Seventh Avenue.
On the park side of the street, the out-of-their-element cowboys Pepper (Woody Harrelson) and Sonny (Kiefer Sutherland) bade farewell to their friend Sam (Ernie Hudson), a cop who longed to be a cowboy, before heading back to New Mexico, in *The Cowboy Way*.

Head east along 59th Street, but not on the park side of the street. [Note: if the tall statue of Christopher Columbus appears to get larger the more you walk, you are heading in the wrong direction]. Continue to 160 Central Park South.

31. 160 Central Park South. Essex House. Upon arriving in New York for his ill-fated rendezvous with Terry (Annette Bening), in *Love Affair*, Mike Gambril (Warren Beatty) checked in here.

The next location has changed names from when it appeared in a movie, but still deserves mention. Continue east and stop at 112 Central Park South.

32. 112 Central Park South. The Westin. In the movie *Regarding Henry*, once cutthroat lawyer Henry Turner (Harrison Ford) struggled to remember his life before he was shot in a holdup. The first word he spoke after his ordeal was "Ritz." He was remembering the Ritz-Carlton, which was the previous name of this hotel. In the movie, Henry went to the hotel and sat in a room, trying to remember his earlier life. An unexpected visit by co-worker Linda (Rebecca Miller) helped Henry remember things he wished he hadn't.

Walk east until you are in front of 50 Central Park South.

33. 50 Central Park South. The St. Moritz Hotel. While dining at the Waldorf-Astoria (see **Walking Tour 7: Midtown**) with his cowboy companion Sonny, Pepper made a big impression on Margaret (Marg Helgenberger) and she invited him to a party, somewhere high up in this hotel, in *The Cowboy Way*.

Walk a little further east until you are across from the entrance to the subway, on the north side of Central Park South, that seems to be built into the stone wall that runs the length of Central Park. Two lanterns adorn the entrance.

34. Central Park South Subway Entrance (between Fifth and Sixth Avenues). Had Woody Harrelson chosen to live on Central Park South, he would have had a very short commute to work each day. In yet another location on this short stretch, Woody found himself here, in *Money Train*. After another "chewing out" by the boss

(Robert Blake), partners and brothers Charlie (Woody) and John (Wesley Snipes) emerged from this staircase and headed east on this street, just as you are doing.

And, sadly, all good things must come to an end, including **Walking Tour 1: 57th Street Shopper's Delight**. So, just as Charlie and John had done in *Money Train*, you should continue east. Pause just before you reach the end of Central Park and note the Oak Room and Bar to your right.

35. Central Park South (west of Fifth Avenue). Plaza Hotel. Oak Room and Bar.

Feel free to head into the famed Oak Room at the Plaza for some coffee, a drink, a snack or a meal. Frank Slade and Charlie did, in *Scent of a Woman*.

------◆------

Continue east until you reemerge at the intersection of Central Park South and Fifth Avenue, with the park on your left and the Plaza Hotel on your right. You have now reached the end of **Walking Tour 1: 57th Street Shopper's Delight**. You are not far from the starting points for several other Walking Tours, including **Walking Tour 2: The (Lower) Upper West Side**, **Walking Tour 4: The Upper East Side** and **Walking Tour 8: Broadway and Beyond**. Be my guest.

Walking Tour 2
THE (LOWER) UPPER WEST SIDE

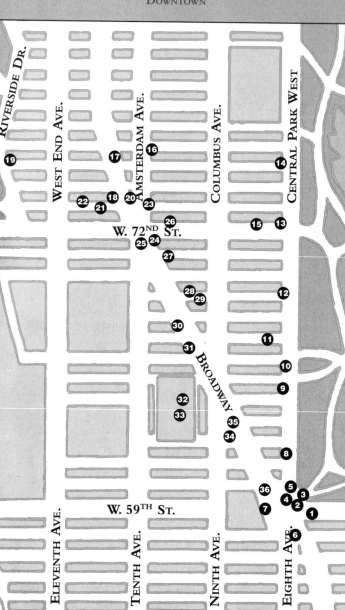

Walking Tour 2
The (Lower) Upper West Side

The Arch in St. Louis, Missouri is meant to symbolize St. Louis as the Gateway to the West (and, presumably, to the East, if one happens to be traveling in the opposite direction) in the United States. By the same token, Columbus Circle has often been called the Gateway to Manhattan's Upper West Side. Renovations completed during the Summer of 1998 have turned the intertwining network of roads into an actual circle, something the configuration lacked for many, many years.

Serviced by a multitude of trains and buses, Columbus Circle is a natural hub and a great place to start **Walking Tour 2**. The starting point is the southeast corner of Columbus Circle, where Central Park South and Broadway come together.

If you choose to get to the starting point by public transportation, you may use any of these subway or bus lines (but the following list is by no means exhaustive):

FROM THE NORTH
SUBWAYS
- **1, 9, B** or **C** southbound to 59th Street/Columbus Circle.

BUSES
- **M5** southbound on Riverside Drive, then Broadway, to Columbus Circle.
- **M7** southbound on Columbus Avenue, then Broadway, to Columbus Circle.

- **M10** southbound on Central Park West to Columbus Circle.
- **M104** southbound on Broadway to Columbus Circle.

FROM THE SOUTH

SUBWAYS

- **1, 9, A, B, C** or **D** northbound to Columbus Circle.
- **N** or **R** northbound to Seventh Avenue and 57th Street. Walk north on Seventh to 59th Street, then left on 59th to Columbus Circle.

BUSES

- **M5** or **M7** northbound on Avenue of the Americas to 59th Street, then westbound on 59th to Columbus Circle.
- **M6** northbound on Avenue of the Americas to 59th Street. Walk west on 59th to Columbus Circle.
- **M10** northbound on Hudson Street, then Eighth Avenue, to Columbus Circle.
- **M104** northbound on Eighth Avenue to Columbus Circle.

FROM THE EAST

SUBWAYS

- **N** or **R** westbound to Seventh Avenue and 57th Street. Walk north on Seventh to 59th Street, then west on 59th to Columbus Circle.
- **7** or **42nd Street Shuttle** to Times Square. Transfer to **1** or **9** northbound to 59th Street/Columbus Circle.

BUSES

- **M31** or **M57** westbound on 57th Street to Broadway. Walk north on Broadway to 59th Street.

FROM THE WEST
BUSES

- **M31** or **M57** eastbound on 57th Street to Broadway. Walk north on Broadway to 59th Street.

As you enter Columbus Circle, you cannot but admire the majestic statue of Christopher Columbus. Towering in the middle of Columbus Circle, it is a good starting point for this Walking Tour.

To begin **Walking Tour 2: The (Lower) Upper West Side**, cross to the south side of Columbus Circle (59th Street) and walk a short distance east until you are standing in front of San Domenico.

1. 240 Central Park South. San Domenico. A very popular and highly-acclaimed restaurant, this is where concierge Doug Ireland (Michael J. Fox) looked through the window to see the woman he liked, Andy (Gabrielle Anwar), having dinner with her married boyfriend, Christian (Anthony Higgins), in *For Love or Money*. Days later, Doug would again look in and, much to his chagrin, see Christian in the restaurant with a different woman.

Return to Columbus Circle and cross over to the northeast corner of Columbus Circle (the entrance to Central Park). Walk a few feet toward the park's entrance, then turn to face Columbus Circle. The lucky TourWalker will find one or more horse-drawn carriages lined along the curb.

2. Central Park West between 59th and 60th Streets. Entrance to Central Park. After a ghostly beast invaded the party he threw for clients instead of friends (so he could write the expense off as a tax deduction), pesky yet well-meaning accountant Louis Tully (Rick Moranis), in *Ghostbusters*, took refuge in Central Park. After being mauled in front of disinterested diners at Tavern on the Green (see **Walking Tour 6: Central Park**), Louis emerged from the park here.

Quite a bit worse for the wear and extremely disheveled after his ordeal, Louis, calling himself Vince Clartho, Keymaster of Gozer, approached a white horse tethered to a carriage at the curb and inquired, "Are you the Gatekeeper?" Chased by the man holding the horse's reins, Louis ran off but not before telling the horse to "wait for the sign, then all prisoners will be released."

Now turn and face the large statue guarding the entrance to the park.

3. Columbus Circle. Central Park Entrance.

In a short period of time, Travis Bickle (Robert DeNiro) went from offering his services as a volunteer for the Presidential campaign of Senator Charles Palatine to considering an assassination of

the man. Sporting a mohawk, Travis looked upon the rally being held right on this spot and made his way through the crowd, hand suspiciously kept inside his jacket. Luckily, he was scared off by the Senator's bodyguards, in *Taxi Driver*.

Walk toward Central Park West. Pause before turning the corner.

4. Columbus Circle and Central Park West. Corner. Look to make sure that book editor Will

Randall (Jack Nicholson) isn't on the prowl, as he was in *Wolf*.

Continue to Central Park West and turn right. Walk the short distance north to the newsstand.

5. Central Park West and 60th Street. Newsstand. Presumably as long-lived as the Empire State Building, this newsstand appeared in the Gene Kelly/Frank Sinatra classic *On the Town*, one of the earlier films filmed entirely on location in New York. Gabey (Gene Kelly) was on a mission to find "Miss Turnstiles," Ivy Smith (Vera Ellen). She boarded a subway and Gabey, Chip (Frank Sinatra) and Ozzie (Jules Munshin) hopped a cab and got out in front of this newsstand. They rushed down the staircase across from the newsstand to find her. But they didn't see Ivy Smith come up the same staircase a moment later and disappear down the street.

Before heading north up Central Park West, look south once more and notice the uniquely designed Two Columbus Circle. Originally an art museum, until recently, it served as home to New York City's Department of Cultural Affairs–Convention and Visitors Bureau.

6. Two Columbus Circle. True *Ghostbusters* aficionados will recognize the building with its arched openings at the top, from the background shot near the end of the movie, where the Stay Puft Marshmallow Man materialized out of the childhood imagination of Ray Stantz (Dan Aykroyd) and began his sticky trek up Central Park West to do battle with Ray, Egon (Harold Ramis) and Peter (Bill Murray).

Now look west, to the far side of Columbus Circle (away from the park).

7. Columbus Circle. Western Boundary. Before they built the New York Coliseum (whose demolition was being planned as this book went to press), there existed a huge billboard on the western perimeter of this circle. In *It Should Happen to You*, Gladys Glover (Judy Holliday) came to New York City to make a name for herself. For $210 a month, she rented the ad space on the billboard that was there and had her name painted in big, bold letters. She made a name for herself and her life was never the same after that.

Cross to the building side of Central Park West and walk north to 61st Street.

8. Central Park West and 61st Street. Mayflower Hotel. After discovering that his wife was having an affair with one of his less palatable colleagues, Will Randall rented a room here, in *Wolf*.

Continue north until you get to 50 Central Park West (CPW), just south of the corner of 65th Street.

9. 50 Central Park West. The Prasada. This beautiful building, with its magnificently carved front pillars, has appeared in at least two movies from recent decades (three, if you count sequels). In the first, *Three Men and a Baby*, the building was home to the playboy triple-threat of Peter (Tom Selleck), Jack (Ted Danson) and Michael (Steve Guttenberg).

In a lesser-known film but, coincidentally, one also starring Steve Guttenberg, *It Takes Two*, the Prasada was home to Steve Guttenberg's wealthy but bitchy fiancée Clarisse (Jane Sibbett, who, by the way, plays Ross's ex-wife on the hit television show "Friends"). In the movie, the incomparable Olsen twins played identical twins, one rich, one poor, who tried to bring together the father of one, Roger Calloway (Guttenberg), with Diane (Kirstie Alley), the camp counselor of the other.

Continue the northward journey on Central Park West until 66th Street.

10. 55 Central Park West. Fans will recognize this building as the home of Dana Barrett (Sigourney Weaver) and Louis Tully (Rick Mora-

nis) in the blockbuster *Ghostbusters*. The corner penthouse of "Spook Central" is where Dana Barrett lived, according to Ray Stantz (Dan Aykroyd). This building was also the crossover point for Zool, Gozer, the Keymaster and the Gatekeeper, as well as all of the other ghosts, ghouls and goblins that invaded New York City in that film. After the final showdown, the ghostbusters emerged from the building onto the damaged street and greeted their adoring and appreciative fans.

The address indicated in the movie was 550, probably a gesture toward privacy for the building's residents, a privacy now shattered. My apologies.

———•◦•———

Continue north on Central Park West to the far side of 67th Street. Turn left on 67th and walk the short distance to 1 West 67th (Café Des Artistes).

11. 1 West 67th Street. Café Des Artistes. After the funeral of their friend, former college chums Annie (Diane Keaton), Elise (Goldie Hawn) and Brenda (Bette Midler) came here to eat, drink and reminisce, in *The First Wives Club*.

———•◦•———

Return to Central Park West and turn left. Head north to 91 Central Park West (corner of 69th Street).

12. 91 Central Park West. Midge Carter (Ossie Davis) had a tough choice to make. He could spend his free time in this building, where he worked the outmoded boiler somewhere down below, or he could venture into Central Park and idle away his time, listening to the ravings of fellow bench-sitter Nat (Walter Matthau). He chose the latter. Otherwise, *I'm Not Rappaport* would have been a much shorter film.

———•◦•———

Walk north on Central Park West until you get to 72nd Street. From the intersection of Central Park West and 72nd Street can be seen one of the best-known buildings in all of New York City, as well as perhaps the most infamous building in the world of rock and roll.

13. 1 West 72nd Street. The Dakota. New York lore has it that the Dakota was named such because, at the time it was built, the wealthy people lived on Fifth Avenue and the new building was so far west it might as well have been in the Dakotas (North or South wasn't specified). Most people, however, know this New York City landmark as the home of John Lennon, and the place where he was gunned down by Mark David Chapman on a cold December night in 1980.

Film buffs will know that demonic forces were at work on Rosemary Woodhouse (Mia Farrow) here in the classic *Rosemary's Baby*.

Rosemary's husband Guy (John Cassavetes) made a pact with the devil, along with his henchmen: neighbors at the Dakota portrayed by Ruth Gordon, Sidney Blackmer, Ralph Bel-

lamy and Patsy Kelly, among others. The film is
a horror classic and Charles Grodin had an early
non-comedy role as Dr. Hill.

Cross 72nd Street to the north side of the street
and continue north until you reach the far side of
75th Street.

**14. 151 Central Park West (at 75th Street).
The Kenilworth.** Stranded in New York,
wanted for murder and with nowhere else to
turn, the hapless foursome Billy (Michael
Keaton), Jack (Peter Boyle), Henry (Christopher
Lloyd) and Albert (Stephen Furst) showed up at
the apartment of Billy's former girlfriend Riley
(Lorraine Bracco), which was in this building, in
The Dream Team.

Turn around and head south on Central Park
West until you again reach 72nd Street. Turn right
on 72nd and head west (away from Central Park).
Although the park is but a stone's throw away, it
doesn't figure prominently in **Walking Tour 2**. It
is the focus of **Walking Tour 6**: **Central Park**,
and is well worth a visit.

Continue walking in a westerly direction (the
Dakota will be on your right). When you reach
the entranceway (marked by a copper-coated
guard booth), you may want to pause for a moment and remember John Lennon, whose life was
tragically taken in this long, darkened corridor on
December 8, 1980.

Continuing west, at 27 West 72nd Street you
will find the Hotel Olcott.

15. 27 West 72nd Street. Hotel Olcott. Having picked up a fare in the then seedy Times
Square area, cab driver Travis Bickle dropped off
the person in front of this hotel, in *Taxi Driver.*

In addition, this is the place where my parents
were married. It may not be a big deal to Tour-

Walkers, but it is a big deal to me, and since it is my book, I beg your indulgence.

———•◆•———

After this brief trip down my memory lane, continue walking west until you get to the corner of Columbus Avenue. Turn right and head north on Columbus. Turn left on 74th Street and head west. Make a right on Amsterdam Avenue and walk north until you reach 75th Street. Cross to the west side of Amsterdam and then turn to look at the building across Amsterdam, near 76th Street.

16. 180 West 76th Street. Riverside Memorial Chapel. Continuously nagged by his overbearing mother, Sheldon (Woody Allen) related a dream he had to his psychiatrist. In the dream, Sheldon's mother (Mae Questel) died and the hearse, with Sheldon driving, pulled away from this building, in the "Oedipus Wrecks" segment of *New York Stories*. True to character, however, his mother was yelling out directions from within the casket in the back of the hearse.

———•◆•———

Head west on 75th Street to Broadway. Look slightly to the right at the bus stop, just north of 75th Street.

17. Broadway, north of 75th Street. Bus Stop. Poor Michael Jordan. No, not *that* Michael Jordan. This Michael Jordan (Gene Wilder) closed a big deal and just wanted someone to celebrate with. Instead, he innocently shared a cab with a mysterious woman, and, next thing he knew, he was being chased as a suspect for a murder he didn't commit. Michael and new friend Kate (Gilda Radner), on the lam in *Hanky Panky*, boarded a bus at this bus stop in an effort to elude capture.

———•◆•———

From the corner of 75th Street, look one block south and diagonally across Broadway. You will notice an architectural beauty, perhaps one of the most stunning residential buildings in all of Manhattan.

Tour 2

18. Broadway and 74th Street (2109 Broadway). The Ansonia.

This imposing structure served as the home of Allie (Bridget Fonda) and her fiancé Sam (Steven Weber), and, for a while, the disruptive Hedra (Jennifer Jason Leigh) in one of those "it could really happen" thrillers, *Single White Female*.

Cross Broadway at 75th Street and head west until you are across from the corner building just before Riverside Drive. The entrance is on 75th Street.

19. 33 Riverside Drive (and 75th Street).

Having just returned from a wonderful vacation at a resort island, Paul Kersey (Charles Bronson) and his wife Joanna (Hope Lange) tried to ease back into their New York City existence. However, their calm was short-lived when three men broke into their apartment, which was in this building, and attacked Joanna and their daughter Carol (Kathleen Tolan), in *Death Wish*.

That Paul should then want revenge for his wife's murder and his daughter's attack does not come as a surprise. What may come as a surprise is that one of the thugs who took part in the attack was Jeff Goldblum. Quite a different role from the intellectual good guys he played in *Jurassic Park* and *Independence Day*.

Return to Broadway (retracing your steps on 75th Street), turn right and head south on Broadway until you get to the corner of Broadway and 74th. The Ansonia should loom directly above you. Look directly across Broadway and you will see the Apple Bank for Savings.

20. 2100 Broadway. Apple Bank for Savings.

A familiar backdrop in television shows and print ads, this building also deserves a NitPick. A NitPick is a factual or geographical discrepancy that occurs in a movie but that is not likely to occur in real life.

In *One Fine Day*, Melanie Parker (Michelle Pfeiffer) and Jack Taylor (George Clooney), after dropping their respective children off at the "Ninth Street Dropoff Center," left the center and walked around the corner. The next shot showed Melanie and Jack walking south on Broadway, next to this Apple Bank building.

Assuming the Ninth Street Dropoff Center is located on 9th Street, some 65 streets south of this spot, which is a reasonable assumption to make, how likely is it that the two of them would have been walking here a few seconds after leaving the dropoff center? My guess is, not very likely, and that, my friends, is a NitPick.

In a city as large as New York, how unlikely is it that a seemingly random location such as Broadway and 74th Street would be used as a movie location for more than one film? If the answer to that question is "pretty unlikely," then how unlikely would it be for the same seemingly random location to be used in two films starring the same actor or actress? I would guess even more unlikely. But that is exactly what happened here.

The movie *One Fine Day* was filmed in 1996. Now, while Michelle Pfeiffer was walking along this stretch of Broadway with co-star George Clooney, did it cross her mind that eight years before, in *Married to the Mob*, she had gotten off the M104 public bus on the corner and walked by this same Apple Bank? Her co-star in that movie, Matthew Modine, did not have the luxury of walking at Michelle's side. In fact, when she got off the bus, Modine, who was trailing her, had to kick out a vent and climb out the top of the bus.

Continue south on Broadway to 73rd Street. Cross 73rd and make a right, heading west until you get to 240 West 73rd Street.

21. 240 West 73rd Street. Proving that an exterior is often nothing more than that, this building was made out to be a hotel, in *Broadway Danny Rose*. After their long sojourn in the swamps of New Jersey, Danny Rose (Woody Allen) and Tina (Mia Farrow) returned to New York. Fearing for Danny should he return to his apartment, because he was being hunted by revenge-seeking brothers, Tina convinced Danny to try and find a hotel room for the night.

They entered the building together. Tina stopped to use the pay phone in the entranceway (not there in real life) and Danny continued on to

the reception desk in the lobby. A peek into the building will reveal a wall of mailboxes where the hotel's desk was purported to be. Told that there were no rooms available, Danny exited the hotel, passing the phone that Tina had used.

Seconds later, outside the hotel, a Cadillac pulled up to the curb and the brothers kidnapped Danny, with Tina already in the trunk.

Walk west another 100 feet or so. Look across 73rd Street at the alleyway next to the Ansonia.

22. Alleyway Next to Ansonia. 73rd Street, West of Broadway. Although the alleyway now leads to an underground parking garage, it was a passage strewn with garbage cans back when Joe Turner (Robert Redford), on his way to meet his CIA colleagues, was shot at instead, in *Three Days of the Condor*.

Head back to Broadway. Cross Broadway until you get to Verdi Square. If construction has made this impossible,[2] head south on Broadway, until roughly halfway down the block toward 72nd Street.

Look slightly north and east, to the corner of Amsterdam Avenue and 73rd Street.

23. 279 Amsterdam Avenue (Northeast Corner of 73rd Street). P & G Bar/Cafe. In *Donnie Brasco*, FBI undercover agent Joe Pistone, *aka* Donnie Brasco (Johnny Depp), took a moment out from his befriending of Lefty Ruggiero (Al Pacino) and his infiltration of the New York City underworld to call his wife from a telephone booth across Amsterdam Avenue from this bar. The telephone booth does not exist in real life, but the bar is a long-standing neighborhood institution.

Continue south (along Verdi Square or Broadway), until reaching 72nd Street.

24. 72nd Street and Amsterdam Avenue. Southeast Corner. Gray's Papaya. In addition to its obvious popularity, judging by the big crowds that surround the place at all hours of the day and night, you might remember that Gray's

---

[2] As this book goes to press, major renovations to the 72nd Street subway station are being planned. If those renovations have begun, it may not be possible to cross Broadway at 73rd Street to get to Verdi Square.

Papaya was a favorite of Alex (Matthew Perry), in *Fools Rush In*. In fact, Gray's Papaya was one of the things that Alex feared he would miss most about New York when he was contemplating forsaking his hometown and moving to Nevada to be with Isabel (Salma Hayek) and their baby to camp out in the desert under the stars.

This eatery is also where Doug Ireland, concierge of the posh Bradbury Hotel (see **Walking Tour 1: 57th Street Shopper's Delight**) took Andy, while keeping her occupied as a favor to one of the hotel's guests, in *For Love or Money*.

More recently, Joe Fox (Tom Hanks) and Kathleen Kelly (Meg Ryan) stopped in here for hot dogs, in *You've Got Mail*.

Without moving, let your eyes drift to the right.

25. 72nd Street Subway Station Entrance.

This entrance has appeared in several movies in recent years. With one glance at the exterior you know why it is such a popular movie location.

Across the street from the subway station entrance, lonely guy Larry (Steve Martin) ran into Jack (Steve Lawrence) who was anything but a lonely guy. Jack was with two very special friends,

Verna (Jolina Collins) and Frieda (Lena Pousette), in *The Lonely Guy*.

In a memorable scene from *Fools Rush In*, Alex, pining away for Isabel, was here confronted by a strange man, a soothsayer perhaps, who hinted at Alex's dilemma and urged him to follow his love, predicting that he would see signs that would show him the way.

Those who prefer more action-oriented films might recall that John McClane (Bruce Willis) and partner-in-adversity Zeus (Samuel L. Jackson) raced to this station and the pay phone to the left of the entrance in order to beat the deadline imposed by the mad bomber Simon (Jeremy Irons), in *Die Hard With a Vengeance*. The pay phone does not exist, but the station itself, as you can see, is very real.

If you are not at Verdi Square, cross Broadway. From Verdi Square, cross Amsterdam Avenue and head east on the north side of 72nd Street until you reach 175.

26. 175 West 72nd Street. In *Mighty Aphrodite*, Lenny (Woody Allen) decided, against the warnings of that film's Greek Chorus, to locate the biological mother of the child that he and his wife Maria (Helena Bonham Carter) had adopted. During his quest, he talked to someone right in front of this building, finding out that his son's birth mother, Linda Ash (Oscar-winner Mira Sorvino), had lived in this building for awhile.

Return to the corner of Amsterdam and 72nd Street. Cross 72nd Street and head south on Broadway. [Note: technically, Amsterdam Avenue begins at 72nd Street. It is an offshoot of Tenth Avenue, which merges with the uptown side of Broadway at 71st Street.] As you walk south, you should be on the east side of Broadway (walking against traffic). At 71st Street, turn left until you are in front of the corner building.

27. 171 West 71st Street. While television reporter Tony Sokalow (Sigourney Weaver) pursued her story, night janitor Daryll (William Hurt) busily pursued her, in *Eyewitness*. One evening, Daryll gave Tony a lift home on his motorcycle to this building, where she lived.

———————

Return to Broadway and then continue south until you get to 69th Street. Turn left on 69th and head east (away from Broadway). This short block bridges the generation gap in film. Stop when you reach 115 West 69th Street.

28. 115 West 69th Street. Gladys Glover came to town to make it big, and while she was here, she lived in this building, along with fellow ten-

ant Pete (Jack Lemmon), a documentary filmmaker, in *It Should Happen to You*.

———————

To jump ahead more than four decades, continue east, stopping just before the corner of Columbus Avenue. On your right, you will notice a small cheese shop. Don't be fooled.

29. 106 West 69th Street. Maya Schaper Cheese & Antiques. A neighborhood institution for years, this picturesque shop was the actual location of the independent book shop owned by Kathleen Kelly and forced out of business by the

opening of a large "chain" bookstore owned by Joe Fox, in *You've Got Mail*. The interior scenes of Kathleen's book shop were also filmed within the store.

———◆·◆———

Retrace your steps to Broadway. Turn left on Broadway and head south to 68th Street. Cross Broadway to get to the west side of the street (walking with traffic). Continue south on Broadway until you reach the enclosed plaza (behind the bus stop).

30. Broadway (between 67th and 68th Streets). Giving up his plum bartending job at a plush resort in Jamaica, Brian Flanagan (Tom Cruise) decided to be a kept man and plaything for the wealthy Bonnie (Lisa Banes), in *Cocktail*. After a while, Brian got sick of the arrangement and tired of being Bonnie's puppy dog. Their big fight and breakup (following Brian's punching out of a sculptor) took place in front of this plaza, after a party for the sculptor, which was held inside.

———◆·◆———

Continue south on Broadway until you are just north of 66th Street. You should be outside the windows of Tower Records, located at 1961 Broadway.

31. Tower Records. 1961 Broadway. Although the original layout was changed when the store was renovated in the mid-1990s, this is the same place where Mickey Sachs (Woody Allen) spotted former sister-in-law and once "really awful and incompatible blind date" Holly (Dianne Wiest), in *Hannah and Her Sisters*. Several years after that disastrous blind date, the former in-laws reunited and discovered that they had much in common.

Continue south until you reach Manhattan's fabled Lincoln Center. Veer off Broadway and continue south on the sidewalk adjacent to Lincoln Center's Avery Fisher Hall until you reach the open plaza area, with the fountain in the center and the Metropolitan Opera House looming majestically in the background. Walk to the far side of the fountain, near the Opera House entrance, and turn to face the fountain.

32. Lincoln Center. The Fountain Plaza. Few can forget sarcastic Peter Venkman in *Ghostbusters*, as he ridiculed a friend of Dana Barrett, referring to "one of the finest musicians in the world" as "the stiff." Pleased that he finally scored a date with Dana, Dr. Venkman, wearing his Ghostbusters' orange, admired the plaza area as the camera focused on a roller skater doing pirouettes near the fountain.

Seventeen years earlier, sitting around this fountain one evening, creative producer Max Bialystock (Zero Mostel) convinced timid accountant Leo Bloom (Gene Wilder) to become his partner and try and produce a Broadway flop, in *The Producers*. After agreeing to join forces, the two men celebrated their new alliance in style.

Cross around to the other side of the fountain and turn to face the imposing Metropolitan Opera House.

33. Lincoln Center. The Metropolitan Opera House.

Finally agreeing to go out with her fiancé's angry brother Ronnie Cammareri (Nicholas Cage), Loretta (Cher) met him for his dream date at the Metropolitan Opera House, for a performance of "La Boheme," in the modern-day love story *Moonstruck*. Looking beautiful in a gorgeous dark maroon gown and with the gray from her hair finally removed, Cher's Loretta was the picture of radiance. The evening turned awkward, yet comical, when Cher bumped into an unlikely acquaintance—her father—but nothing could destroy the magic of the evening for Loretta and Ronnie.

Similarly, at the end of *The Secret of My Success*, new couples Brantley Foster (Michael J. Fox) and Christy Wills (Helen Slater) and Fred Melrose (John Pankow) and Vera Prescott (Margaret Whitton) attended the opera, while their limousine awaited their return in a very unlikely spot—right next to this fountain.

With only a few more stops to make and a few blocks left to travel, it is time to head out of Lincoln Center. If you are lucky enough to be taking **Walking Tour 2**: **The (Lower) Upper West Side** during the December holiday season, you can stand at the top of the steps leading to Lincoln Center and admire the beautiful Christmas tree, adorned with its musical instruments.

When you've finished taking in the aura of this magical part of Manhattan, head down the stairs leading to Columbus Avenue, and turn right, walking to the corner (the first traffic light you come to). If you have made it all the way to 62nd Street, you have gone too far.

At Columbus Avenue and 63rd Street, cross Columbus Avenue. You should be directly across from 48 West 63rd Street. The current establishment at that location is a restaurant called Merlot, with the Iridium Jazz Club on the lower level. However, the location prior to such occupants had a storied cinematic history.

34. 48 West 63rd Street. In the television series "Friends," Monica Geller worked as a chef at Merlot.

In 1989's *Sea of Love*, Frank Keller (Al Pacino) and Sherman Touhey (John Goodman) played New York City cops who went undercover to capture a serial killer believed to be preying on

forlorn "personals ad" respondents. They set up a sting operation at this location which, at the time, was the long-standing New York City tavern O'Neal's Balloon. At a table not far from the window onto 63rd Street, first Keller and then Touhey posed as "personals ad" placers, and met, one after another, those who responded to the ads. One of the women answering Keller's ad was the beautiful, sexy, sultry Helen (Ellen Barkin).

———•◆•———

Before leaving this intersection, it may interest you to know that you are standing on the exact spot where Alvie Singer (Woody Allen) parted ways with Annie Hall (Diane Keaton) at the very end of *Annie Hall*.

Continuing east on 63rd Street (away from Columbus Avenue and Lincoln Center), you will come to the corner of Broadway and 63rd Street.

35. 63rd Street and Broadway. Even after Aunt Celeste (Sally Field) had warned Lori Craven (Elisabeth Shue) against moving to New York and pursuing a career as an actress, Lori had done just that, in *Soapdish*. Thanks primarily to some poor choices, every life Aunt Celeste had touched had been brought to the brink of ruin. Bemoaning the horrible things she had done, Celeste poured her heart out to best friend Rose (Whoopi Goldberg), who also happened to be one of the writers on the soap opera "The Sun Also Sets," of which Celeste was the star. Their dialogue took place on this corner at 63rd Street and Broadway, and it is here that Celeste stepped off the curb and stood bravely in front of an oncoming bus, hoping to end it all.

———•◆•———

Head south on Broadway. Fans of the New York City classic *Taxi Driver* will be interested to know that on the southeast corner of Broadway and 62nd Street (a plot of land that has been vacant for many, many years), stood the political headquarters staffed by Betsy (Cybill Shepherd) and visited frequently by Travis Bickle.

***

With the end in sight, we continue south on Broadway until we reach the northern boundary of Columbus Circle (at 60th Street). Look halfway across Broadway, to the subway entrance on the middle island of concrete, between the uptown and downtown traffic lanes.

36. Broadway and 60th Street. Subway Entrance. Thinking that Sue Charlton (Linda Kozlowski) had agreed to marry another man, Mick Dundee (Paul Hogan) went for a walkabout on the streets of New York before returning to his native Australia. He descended this staircase in *"Crocodile" Dundee*. A few minutes later, Sue, racing to catch him, removed her shoes along Central Park South and continued her pursuit barefoot. She crossed Columbus Circle and descended the same staircase.

***

As you walk through Columbus Circle, you can admire once again the central statue of Christopher Columbus which, though towering, is dwarfed by the large buildings around the Circle's perimeter.

Walking Tour 2: The (Lower) Upper West Side ends at this point. However, you are in close proximity to the starting point for **Walking Tour 1: 57th Street Shopper's Delight** and but a stone's throw from the beginning of **Walking Tour 8: Broadway and Beyond**.

Walking Tour 3
THE (UPPER) UPPER WEST SIDE

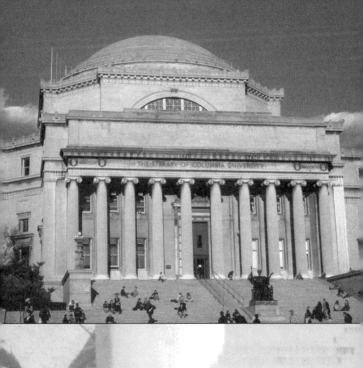

Walking Tour 3
THE (UPPER) UPPER WEST SIDE

or purposes of these Walking Tours only, the (Upper) Upper West Side begins where the (Lower) Upper West Side leaves off. There is no actual separation between the two zones, but because scenes from so many films have been shot on the Upper West Side, it is easier and less time-consuming for the TourWalker to cover each area separately.

As indicated on the above map, the (Upper) Upper West Side stretches from 75th Street all the way up to the area of Columbia University (around 116th Street). This Walking Tour is slightly longer than the others, and may take the Tour-Walker 2 and 1/4 hours, but don't blame me. Blame those responsible for the movie *You've Got Mail*. You'll see what I mean.

Walking Tour 3: The (Upper) Upper West Side begins at 116th Street and Broadway, in front of the entrance to Columbia University. If you choose to get to the starting point by public transportation, you may use any of the following subway or bus lines (although the following list is by no means exhaustive):

FROM THE NORTH
SUBWAYS
• **1** or **9** southbound to 116th Street.
BUSES
• **M4** or **M104** southbound on Broadway to 116th Street.

- **M5** southbound on Broadway, then River-side Drive, to 116th Street. Walk east on 116th to Broadway.

FROM THE SOUTH
SUBWAYS
- **1** or **9** northbound to 116th Street.
BUSES
- **M5** northbound on Broadway, then River-side Drive, to 116th Street. Walk east on 116th to Broadway.
- **M104** northbound to 116th Street.

FROM THE EAST
BUSES
- **M4** northbound on Madison Avenue, then westbound on 110th Street, then northbound on Broadway, to 116th Street.
- **M66, M72, M79, M86** or **M96** westbound to Broadway. Transfer to **M104** northbound on Broadway, to 116th Street.

If you have maneuvered correctly, you should be right in front of the first location of **Walking Tour 3: The (Upper) Upper West Side**, the east side of Broadway, at 116th Street.

1. 116th Street and Broadway. Columbia University. One of the most prestigious academic institutions in the United States. Columbia's beautiful campus has appeared in several films. Enter the gates to the campus and walk east until you are in the open plaza area, with impressive-looking buildings all around.

Before getting their funding revoked and getting thrown off campus, Peter Venkman (Bill Murray), Ray Stantz (Dan Aykroyd) and Egon Spengler (Harold Ramis), in *Ghostbusters*, worked here at Columbia. After they were booted from their office, they sat out on the university's grounds and pondered their next move.

In a more recent film, *The Mirror Has Two Faces*, both Rose Morgan (Barbra Streisand) and Greg Larkin (Jeff Bridges) were professors at Columbia. Several scenes in the film took place on these memorable and picturesque grounds.

Exit the same gate at Broadway and 116th Street. Cross Broadway to the west side of the Street. Head south (do not cross 116th Street) until you reach the corner of 112th Street. Look across Broadway. If it hasn't jumped out at you by now, then you probably are not a true "Seinfeld" devotee.

2. 2880 Broadway (at 112th Street). Tom's Restaurant. This well-known facade from the long-running television show sits at the corner of Broadway and 112th Street. Now you may ask why, if Jerry and Kramer lived on 81st Street (a

fact often referred to on the show), did they frequent the "coffee shop" on 112th Street, a full mile-and-a-half away? Considering that not too many New Yorkers would travel such a distance to eat on a daily basis, it is a fair question.

Continue heading south on Broadway. At 107th Street, Broadway veers left and West End Avenue begins. Bear left and stay on Broadway, continuing south. When you get to 105th Street, slow down until you reach the tavern in the middle of the next block.

3. 2731 Broadway. Tap A Keg. After Michael (Daniel Stern) got dumped by his wife, he and Phillip (Ben Masters) hoisted a few, then wheeled their bicycles out of this venerable tavern, in *Key Exchange*.

Continue south until you reach 100th Street. Slow down but continue walking until you are halfway down the next block. Look directly across Broadway.

4. Broadway, between 100th and 99th Streets. The Metro. This longstanding movie house was the site of redemption for Mickey Sachs (Woody Allen), in *Hannah and Her Sisters*. Having fallen to the depths of despair, wondering if there was anything worth living for, questioning the meaning of life, and even having tried (unsuccessfully) to end it all, Mickey wandered the streets of the (Upper) Upper West Side and ended up in this movie house. The film being shown at the time was the Marx Brothers classic, *Duck Soup*, and, watching it, Mickey came to realize that maybe life didn't have to have some deep-seated meaning after all. It may be enough just to be alive. Renewed and reborn, Mickey eventually left the theatre and picked up the pieces of his life, finding happiness in the un-likeliest of places along the way.

Continue south on Broadway and turn right on 94th Street. Walk halfway down the block, until you get to the stone and brick archway on the right.

5. 265 West 94th Street. Pomander Walk.

A breathtakingly serene respite from the hustle and bustle of Manhattan, this charming block of small houses was one of the locations on the architectural tour of the city given to Holly (Dianne Wiest) and April (Carrie Fisher) by David (Sam Waterston), the architect whom the two friends

and business partners had met at a party and were about to fight over, in *Hannah and Her Sisters.*

Unfortunately, the gate is locked because the short street is private, but you can get a glimpse of the houses on either side of the walkway beyond the wrought-iron fence.

Continue west on 94th Street (the same direction that got you to Pomander Walk) until you reach West End Avenue. Turn left on West End and head south until you reach 92nd Street. Cross 92nd and look diagonally across the street.

6. West End Avenue and 92nd Street. Northwest Corner. Troubled writer Harry (Woody Allen) was being honored at his old school, and wanted to bring his son along for the occasion. But that would require taking the boy out of school and getting the consent of his ex-wife Joan (Kirstie Alley), in *Deconstructing Harry*. Harry confronted Joan and they ended up bickering on this corner. Harry lost the argument.

An interesting note about this film. Visiting his son's school, Harry talked with his son while a mother sitting at the next table eavesdropped on the conversation. She was played by Mariel Hemingway, who had appeared as a young love interest of Woody Allen's in an earlier film, *Manhattan* (see **Walking Tour 4: The Upper East Side**).

Turn left and head west on 92nd Street to Riverside Drive. Turn left on Riverside and head south to 91st Street.
If it is spring or summer and it is daylight, it may be worth venturing into Riverside Park here to see the community garden where Joe Fox and Kathleen Kelly shared a very special moment. If you choose, enter the park at 91st Street and follow the path down, bearing left as the path forks. The playground should be on your left. The path lets out, up a slight incline, at the garden.

7. Riverside Park at 91st Street. Community Garden. They started out disliking each other, then the ice melted and they developed a mutual attraction. But it was too late. Kathleen Kelly (Meg Ryan) was going to meet her e-mail pal here at the community garden. During spring and summer, the garden is in full bloom, as it was at the end of *You've Got Mail*, when Joe Fox (Tom Hanks) showed up and foiled Kathleen's rendezvous. Or did he? As their eyes met, Kathleen was moved to tears, Joe's loyal dog Brinkley scampered nearby, and someone began singing about

something being somewhere over the rainbow.

If you entered Riverside Park, return up the path to Riverside Drive. If not, you should still be at 91st Street. Continue south on Riverside Drive (the park should remain on your right) until halfway between 89th Street and 88th Street. Note the monument on your right.

8. Riverside Drive (near 89th Street). Soldiers' and Sailors' Memorial Monument.

They may have been the least likely of roommates, but they were still best of friends. One evening, Oscar Madison (Walter Matthau) and

Felix Unger (Jack Lemmon) sat near this monument and talked, in the movie version of *The Odd Couple.*

Continue south to 131 Riverside Drive (at 85th Street).

9. 131 Riverside Drive (at 85th Street). After sitting on the bench, Oscar and Felix came back here, where they lived, in *The Odd Couple*. This building is not to be confused, however, with the apartment in the television series of the same name (see **Walking Tour 4: The Upper East Side**).

Continue south on Riverside Drive and turn left at 84th Street. Head east until you get back to West End Avenue.

Tour 3

10. 505 West End Avenue (at 84th Street). Back to *The Mirror Has Two Faces*, this building is where Rose went to live with her mother (Lauren Bacall) after leaving husband Greg. A highly memorable scene at the end of the film had Rose and Greg waltzing outside the building, here on West End Avenue.

Cross West End Avenue and head east for two blocks, until you reach Amsterdam Avenue. Turn left and go north on Amsterdam until you get halfway between 86th and 87th streets. Look directly across Amsterdam Avenue.

11. 541 Amsterdam Avenue. Barney Greengrass. Time for a NitPick. (If you are not sure what constitutes a NitPick, see the example given in **Walking Tour 2: The (Lower) Upper West Side**, Location 20). In the movie *Smoke*, Auggie (Harvey Keitel) managed a smokeshop somewhere in the heart of Brooklyn. He befriended Paul (William Hurt), a man who had suffered greatly. Near the end of the movie, they decided to leave the store and get something to eat, mainly because Auggie wanted to tell Paul a nice Christmas story. To get some food they ended up here, in Manhattan, at Barney Greengrass, famous for such delicacies as smoked salmon, sturgeon and whitefish.

Is the food good? Absolutely. But is it likely that these two guys would come here all the way from Brooklyn, when the movie suggests that they were just going nearby to get a bite? If you don't think so, then you know what a NitPick is.

Because it was in the neighborhood, it made more sense for Kathleen and Birdie (Jean Stapleton) to share a meal here, which they did, in *You've Got Mail*.

Continue up Amsterdam until you get to 89th Street. Turn right and walk the short distance until you are in front of 174-6. Note the building directly across 89th Street.

12. 175 West 89th Street. Claremont Riding Academy. Every good movie featuring good guys and bad guys has to have a final showdown. In *Eyewitness*, the final showdown between night janitor Daryll (William Hurt) and bad guy Joseph (Christopher Plummer) occurred here, with horses running amok.

Walk left and return to Amsterdam Avenue. Turn left and head south on Amsterdam until you reach 83rd Street.

13. 477 Amsterdam Avenue (at 83rd Street). Hi-Life Bar & Grill. Poor Ray (Campbell Scott). Every bartender in town seemed to owe him money and, before he could lend his sister money, he had to make the rounds and call in his debts. Ray was a bartender here, and before the night was over he was to come across some old faces and some new, including his ex-girlfriend Maggie (Daryl Hannah), his sister's worthless boyfriend Jimmy (Eric Stoltz) and a bookie named Fatty (Charles Durning), in a movie, named after the bar, called *Hi-Life*.

Head south on Amsterdam until you reach the restaurant just before 81st Street, on the northeast corner.

14. 441 Amsterdam Avenue (at 81st Street). Louie's.

Kathleen Kelly and Frank Navasky (Greg Kinnear) had both realized that they were not in love with each other. The only thing left to do was let the other person know, which they did while sitting at a table inside this restaurant, in *You've Got Mail*.

Cross to the west side of Amsterdam and turn right. Head north on Amsterdam to the far side of 83rd Street. Make a left on 83rd and walk the short distance until you are in front of Cafe Lalo, yet another location from *You've Got Mail*.

15. 201 West 83rd Street. Cafe Lalo.

Kathleen was here, book and flower in hand, ready to meet her secret e-mail pal. And then Joe had to show up and ruin things. But Joe knew something that Kathleen didn't, and moviegoers knew something that neither Kathleen nor Joe discovered until the end of *You've Got Mail*.

Return to Amsterdam and make a left. Walk north to 86th Street, then make a right on 86th and walk east until you reach Central Park West. Turn right and stop at the first building on the corner.

16. 257 Central Park West. Orwell House.

Ruthless financier Lawrence Garfield (Danny DeVito) finally met his match. Beautiful, sexy, smart, and a lawyer, she was also the daughter of the head of the company that Lawrence intended to take over. Her name was Kate (Penelope Ann Miller) and she lived here, in *Other Peoples' Money*.

Head south on Central Park West until you reach the Museum of Natural History (81st Street). Look west along 81st Street (away from Central Park).

17. 81st Street, west of Central Park West.

Getting to know one another, Judy (Mia Farrow)

and Michael (Liam Neeson) strolled along this street, in *Husbands and Wives*.

Continue south on Central Park West to the museum's entrance (behind the statue of Theodore Roosevelt).

18. Museum of Natural History. Central Park West and 79th Street.

Still trying to find Mrs. Lieberman, the woman who could prove his allegations about sanitation industry corruption and hopefully save his job, Jack Taylor (George Clooney), talking into his cell phone, brought his daughter Maggie (Mae Whitman) and Maggie's schoolmate Sammy (Alex D. Linz), the son of Melanie Parker (Michelle Pfeiffer), to this Museum, in *One Fine Day*.

The Museum is also where Walter Kornbluth (Eugene Levy) was first ridiculed when he revealed that he had seen a mermaid with his own

eyes. Later on, when the mermaid, Madison (Daryl Hannah), was captured and brought in for testing, Dr. Kornbluth received the respect he so craved. All of this occurred against the wishes of Allan Bauer (Tom Hanks), who had a less scientific, more romantic interest in the mermaid. And all of this happened in *Splash*.

Continue south to the end of the Musuem, and turn right on 77th Street. Walk west until you reach the South Entrance to the Museum, on 77th Street.

19. Museum of Natural History. 77th Street Entrance. On the eve of Thanksgiving, this street is blocked off as balloons for the legendary Macy's Thanksgiving Day Parade are inflated and kept overnight. The event has turned into one of New York's most festive of the year, and is well worth a visit. In the movie, *Miracle on 34th Street* the start of the parade was captured on film, and began on this very street, in front of the Museum's entrance. It was here that Kris Kringle (Edmund Gwenn) discovered that the Santa Claus who was scheduled to ride on one of the floats was drunk and had to be replaced. Which he was.

In another film, Alonzo (Harvey Keitel) pulled

up in front of this entrance and confronted Randy (Molly Ringwald) to collect on a debt, in *The Pick-Up Artist.*

Look across the street to 20 West 77th Street.

20. 20 West 77th Street. In a car parked right at the curb where you are standing, writer of detective novels Phillip accompanied a real detective (Danny Aiello) on an actual stakeout, in *Key Exchange.* The building they were watching is 20 West 77th Street.

Continue west on 77th Street and turn left on Columbus Avenue. If you are a fan of the television show "Seinfeld," you may recognize the restaurant on the southeast corner of Columbus and 77th Street. Isabella's has appeared several times in the show, as a place where the "fab four" has gone on the occasional dinner date.

Walk south one block until you reach the corner of 76th Street. Turn to the left.

21. 76th Street, east of Columbus Avenue. Lonely guy Larry Hubbard (Steve Martin) decided to make one last effort to avoid a life of utter loneliness and to try and win back his true love, Iris (Judith Ivey), who was about to marry Jack (Steve Lawrence), in *The Lonely Guy.* Beginning his mad dash to the church to stop the wedding, Larry rushed from his apartment and headed west from under the awning of this Chinese restaurant to catch a cab on Columbus Avenue.

Cross 76th Street and head slightly east until you reach 60 West 76th.

22. 60 West 76th Street. This building was the home of Bronte (Andie MacDowell) and, for the purposes of fooling immigration officers, her "husband" Georges (Gerard Depardieu), in *Green Card*. Fans of the movie will remember the curved staircase leading up from the lobby, easily visible from the street.

Return to Columbus and turn left, walking south one block to 75th Street. Cross 75th and turn left.

23. 60 West 75th Street. New York casanova Jack Jericho (Robert Downey, Jr.) had spotted Randy Jensen and approached her, using his best lines and proving that he was, in fact, a pick-up artist of the highest order, in *The Pick-Up Artist*. They turned the very corner where you are now standing and stopped in front of this first building. Having told her she had the face of a Botticelli and the body of a Degas, Jack did surprisingly well with Randy. And many other women.

Look directly across Columbus Avenue, to the restaurant on the corner.

24. 316 Columbus Avenue (at 75th Street). Pappardella. Observant fans of "Seinfeld" will recognize this recurring restaurant exterior (although it was recently painted the existing colors, rather than the green and white when it appeared in the show), as another site of the occasional meal and date for the Seinfeld four.

Cross Columbus Avenue to the west side of the street, turn right and head north up Columbus until you are between 78th and 79th Streets.

25. 384 Columbus Avenue. Ocean Grill. Kathleen was trying to figure out the identity of her e-mail paramour and enemy-turned-friend Joe was only too happy to help, in *You've Got*

Mail. While eating lunch here, they tried to decipher the meaning of the screen name "NY 152".

Turn back and head south on Columbus to 78th Street. Turn right.

26. 78th Street. Just West of Columbus Avenue. Briefly considering heroics, New York thespian Elliot Garfield (Richard Dreyfuss) chased a car down this street to retrieve groceries the men in the car had stolen from Elliot's roommate, Paula (Marsha Mason), in Neil Simon's *The Goodbye Girl.* Just before reaching the corner, the men got out of the car brandishing a weapon. Sensing that his strength lay more in his acting ability than his fists, Elliot dropped his own groceries and beat a hasty retreat.

Tour 3

Walk west on 78th Street. Stop in front of the building on the left, just before the corner.

27. 170 West 78th Street. Within the confines of this building, thanks to the insensitivity of their mutual acquaintance, Elliot and Paula were thrown together as roommates. Although it sounds like *The Odd Couple*, it is really *The Goodbye Girl* again.

Continue west on 78th Street until you reach Broadway. Cross to the west side of Broadway, and turn right. Walk north until you are in front of the beautiful building named the "Apthorp."

28. Broadway between 78th and 79th Streets. The Apthorp. With another of those beautifully designed facades that seem to be prevalent on Manhattan's Upper West Side, the Apthorp was home to Allison, a friend of the mayor's daughter, Bernadette (Mary Elizabeth Mastrantonio), in *The January Man.* The friend was murdered and, for reasons somehow made clear in the film, the job of solving the crime fell on the shoulders of Nick Starkey (Kevin Kline).

———◆·◆———

Walk north a few more yards until you are standing near the entrance to the subway station.

29. Broadway and 79th Street. Subway Entrance.

29. Broadway and 79th Street. Subway Entrance. After discovering that his friend George (Ricky Jay) had been murdered, and knowing that he would be blamed, passive Joe (Campbell Scott) climbed out the window of George's apartment and entered the subway down this staircase, just as the cops were racing to George's building, in *The Spanish Prisoner*.

———◆·◆———

Walk north on Broadway until you reach the near corner of 80th Street. Look across Broadway.

30. Broadway and 80th Street. Starbucks. They used to go here separately to get their morning coffee, but then they became friends and Kathleen and Joe sat here together, in *You've Got Mail*.

———◆·◆———

Continue north on Broadway until you reach the entrance to Zabar's, half a block up.

31. 2245 Broadway (between 80th and 81st Streets). Zabar's. This popular West Side food institution (go in and try not to buy anything: I dare you) is where Kathleen found herself on the cash-only checkout line, with too little cash, and Joe came to her rescue, in *You've Got Mail*.

———◆·◆———

You have now reached the last location on **Walking Tour 3: The (Upper) Upper West Side**.

Walking Tour 4
THE UPPER EAST SIDE

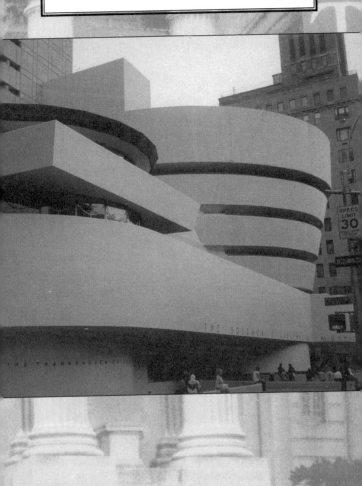

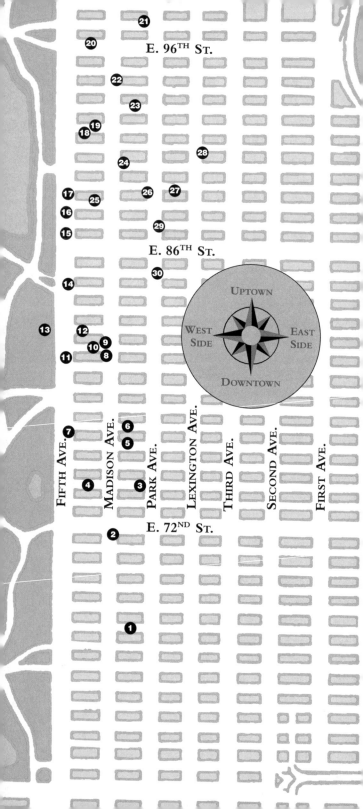

Walking Tour 4

THE UPPER EAST SIDE

The Upper East Side has been synonymous with elegance and old money for a long time. Not surprisingly, many of the locations on **Walking Tour 4: The Upper East Side** consist of elegant buildings that adorn Fifth Avenue and Park Avenue and that have been used as exteriors of homes of New York City's elite—the movers and shakers who live in apartments much larger than those most of us have ever seen.

Walking Tour 4: The Upper East Side begins at 67th Street and Madison Avenue. If you choose to get to the starting point by public transportation, you may use any of the following subway or bus lines (although the following list is by no means exhaustive):

FROM THE NORTH
SUBWAYS
- **4, 5** or **6** southbound to 86th Street. Switch to **6** southbound to 68th Street. Walk west on 68th to Madison Avenue, then south on Madison to 67th Street.

BUSES
- **M1, M2, M3** or **M4** southbound on Fifth Avenue to 67th Street. Walk east on 67th to Madison Avenue.
- **M101, M102** or **M103** southbound on Lexington Avenue to 67th Street. Walk west on 67th to Madison Avenue.

FROM THE SOUTH
SUBWAYS

- **4, 5** or **6** northbound to 59th Street. Switch to **6** northbound to 68th Street. Walk west on 68th to Madison Avenue, then south on Madison to 67th Street.

- **B** or **Q** northbound to Lexington Avenue and 63rd Street. Walk west on 63rd to Madison Avenue, then north on Madison to 67th Street.

BUSES

- **M1, M2** or **M3** northbound on Park Avenue South, then Park Avenue, then Madison Avenue, to 67th Street.

- **M4** northbound on Madison Avenue to 67th Street.

- **M101, M102** or **M103** northbound on Third Avenue to 67th Street. Walk west on 67th to Madison Avenue.

FROM THE EAST
BUSES

- **M66** westbound on 67th Street to Madison Avenue.

- **M72** westbound on 72nd Street to Fifth Avenue, then southbound on Fifth to 67th Street. Walk east on 67th to Madison Avenue.

FROM THE WEST
BUSES

- **M66** or **M72** eastbound to Madison Avenue and 67th Street.

- **M79, M86** or **M96** eastbound to Fifth Avenue. Transfer to **M1, M2, M3** or **M4** southbound on Fifth, to 67th Street. Walk east on 67th to Madison Avenue.

To begin **Walking Tour 4: The Upper East Side**, you should be standing at the intersection of Madison Avenue and 67th Street. To get there, if you took public transportation that left you at Fifth Avenue and 67th Street, walk east one block to Madison. Now, everyone, walk east on 67th Street the very short distance until you are standing in front of 27 East 67th.

1. 27 East 67th Street. Ronaldo Maia Flowers. After an overnight stakeout, New York City detective "Popeye" Doyle (Gene Hackman) followed the elusive Frenchman (Fernando Rey) and waited outside this store while the Frenchman attended to some business within, in *The French Connection*.

Return to Madison and turn right. Walk north on Madison to 72nd Street. The next stop is the elegant building on the southeast corner of the intersection of Madison Avenue and 72nd Street.

2. 867 Madison Avenue. Ralph Lauren Store. Southeast Corner. Thanks to the magic potion of Dr. Yang, Alice's herbalist, Alice (Mia Farrow), newly invisible, decided to follow two well-known gossips into this store, in *Alice*. She overheard their conversation and realized that her affair with Joe (Joe Mantegna) was not as secret as she had hoped. She also learned that her husband Doug (William Hurt) had had his own infidelities, which everyone also seemed to know about. Joe, also invisible, accompanied Alice into the store, but he had a different agenda. Spotting supermodel Elle MacPherson, Joe followed her into the dressing room. A few minutes later, Elle came out to complain to a salesclerk about "heavy breathing" coming from somewhere inside the changing room.

Head east on 72nd Street one block, to Park Avenue. Turn left on Park and head north to the far corner of 74th Street.

3. 800 Park Avenue. Sherman McCoy (Tom Hanks) had it all. As a self-described Master of the Universe, McCoy had a high-paying job as a trader on Wall Street, an expensive lifestyle, a beautiful mistress at his beck and call [Note: for the apartment of the mistress, see **Walking Tour 5: The Far East**], a beautiful wife and a child with whom he lived in a lavish multilevel apartment in this building. That is, before it all started to unravel, in *The Bonfire of the Vanities*.

——————

Head west on 74th Street (away from Park Avenue). Cross Madison Avenue and continue until you reach 4 East 74th.

4. 4 East 74th Street. His sister Savannah finally on the road to recovery, high school football coach Tom Wingo (Nick Nolte) waited outside, across the street from this building, in *The Prince*

of Tides. Inside was the office of Dr. Susan Lowenstein (Barbra Streisand) and as she emerged, Tom hesitated, suspecting Lowenstein would not want to hear his news. But the perceptive Dr. Lowenstein knew before Tom opened his mouth that he had decided to return home to South Carolina and his family.

——————

Retrace your steps back to Madison Avenue.

Turn left on Madison and walk north the two blocks to 76th Street.

5. 35 East 76th Street (at Madison Avenue). Carlyle Restaurant. The movie is *Hannah and Her Sisters*. Mickey Sachs (Woody Allen) was in the middle of the worst date of his life with former sister-in-law Holly (Dianne Wiest). Trying to infuse a little culture into the evening, Mickey took Holly to the Cafe Carlyle to hear Bobby Short sing. Holly was more at home in the world of punk rock, and the two clashed miserably. At least at the time.

Continue north on Madison to 77th Street. Turn right and walk a few steps until you are across from 55 East 77th Street.

6. 55 East 77th Street. Joe Turner (Robert Redford) left this building to get some lunch and when he returned to his company's offices, he discovered that every one of his CIA colleagues had been brutally murdered, in *Three Days of the Condor*.

Head back the other way (west) on 77th Street until you get to Fifth Avenue. Turn left on Fifth and stop in front of the building on the corner.

7. 956 Fifth Avenue. Dr. Henry Harrison (William Hurt) lived in this building and Beatrice (Juliette Binoche) lived in Paris, but they temporarily traded apartments, with Henry staying in Paris and Beatrice staying in Henry's apartment here, in *A Couch in New York*.

Walk north on Fifth Avenue (Central Park should be on your left) to 78th Street. Turn right on 78th and head east to Madison Avenue. At Madison, turn left and walk north to 1064 Madison, just past 80th Street.

8. 1064 Madison Avenue (between 80th and 81st Streets). E.A.T.

Usually out of the city on weekends, sisters Lane (Gaby Hoffmann) and Laura (Natalie Portman) spent a rare day in New York. They ventured into this delicatessen and bake shop and spotted Jeffrey (John Griffin), on whom they both had a crush, in *Everyone Says I Love You*. The good news—Jeffrey was heir to the Vandermost millions, so he was quite a catch. The bad news—he could only choose one of them.

Continue up Madison to 81st Street. Cross to the far side of 81st Street.

9. 1076 Madison Avenue (at 81st Street). Frank E. Campbell Funeral Chapel.

Little did they realize it at the time, but the suicide of their friend Cynthia Griffin (Stockard Channing) would reunite college friends Brenda (Bette Midler), Annie (Diane Keaton) and Elise (Goldie Hawn) and spur them to action and renewed friendship, in *The First Wives Club*. Cynthia's funeral was held here, one of the most famous funeral parlors in New York.

Poor Goldie Hawn. That same year, she had to say goodbye to another family member at this funeral home. However, this other funeral ended on a more chipper note. In *Everyone Says I Love You*, the family gathered to pay their last respects to Grandpa (Patrick Cranshaw). While there, the family wondered about the frailty and meaning of life and, lo and behold, the ghost of Grandpa sat up in the coffin. Grandpa's ghost broke into song and dance in an effort to perk up the mourners.

He was joined by other ghosts, and the revelry even spilled out onto the street, right where you are now standing.

And while the actual location was not shown, it was Campbell's that Blake (Robert Downey, Jr.) called, aided by one of his girlfriends, Carla (Heather Graham), to make funeral arrangements for his mother, in *Two Girls and a Guy*.

Head west on 81st Street a few steps to 15 East 81st.

10. 15 East 81st Street. Sidney (Alan Alda) and Constance (Allison Janney) Miller threw a dinner party in their apartment in this building. At the party, Sidney's daughter Nina (Jennifer Aniston) first met George (Paul Rudd) who, however ill-suited, was to become the object of her affection. She also met Dr. Robert Joley (Tim Daly), who revealed to her that he and George shared an apartment but that George would soon be asked to find a new place to live, in *The Object of My Affection*.

Continue west on 81st until you get to Fifth Avenue. Turn left and stop in front of 995 Fifth.

11. 995 Fifth Avenue. Stanhope Hotel. Beth (Anne Heche) stayed here while she was in New York trying to convince Sheriff (Vince Vaughn) and Tony (David Conrad) to return to Malaysia and agree to serve time in prison, so that Lewis (Joaquin Phoenix) would not be hanged, in *Return to Paradise*.

Head north on Fifth Avenue to 82nd Street. Turn right on 82nd and stop in front of the building on the corner.

12. 1009 Fifth Avenue (at 82nd Street). This elegant building was home to the Turner family in *Regarding Henry*: Henry (Harrison Ford), the high-powered attorney, whose life was turned around when he was shot by a gunman (played by John Leguziamo) while out to pick up a pack of cigarettes; Sarah (Annette Bening), his beleaguered wife; and Rachel (Mikki Allen), the 11-year old daughter who almost lost her mean and nasty father that fateful night but got something better in the end: a kinder and gentler father. Oh, and let's not forget their dog, Buddy.

This building served as the setting of another wealthy home, in *The First Wives Club*. Out for revenge on their ex-husbands or soon-to-be ex-husbands, Elise, Brenda and Annie enlisted the help of their friend, society doyenne Gunilla Goldberg (Maggie Smith). Gunilla, herself a "first wife" many times over, was only too happy to help, and invited Shelly (Sarah Jessica Parker), the current girlfriend of Brenda's ex, Morty (Dan Hedaya), for a society lunch.

Proving that it has stood the test of time, the building also appeared in *The French Connection*. The police tailed one of the suspects in the drug smuggling ring to this building, and discussed the fact that Don Ameche, the actor, lived within.

Tour 4

Now, turn back toward Fifth and admire the venerable entrance to the Metropolitan Museum of Art.

13. Fifth Avenue and 82nd Street. Metropolitan Museum of Art.

In the 1980 thriller *Dressed to Kill*, bored housewife Kate Miller (Angie Dickinson) wandered the rooms of this museum, playing cat-and-mouse with a mysterious man. She alternated between running from him and chasing him. Frustrated by the failure of her search through the various galleries and having lost her glove, Kate exited the museum and proceeded down these stairs.

At the foot of the stairs, she noticed a hand

dangling her glove from the backseat of a taxicab sitting at the curb. Viewers of the movie, along with the cabdriver, will never forget the scene that followed Kate's being pulled into the backseat. It is a lesson that could be learned by many filmmakers of today. Often just the suggestion of sex is far more erotic than explicit love scenes.

The museum was also the site of a gala affair that Steven Taylor (Michael Douglas) and his young wife Emily (Gwyneth Paltrow) attended,

in *A Perfect Murder*. Little did Steven know at the time that the artist David Shaw (Viggo Mortensen), for whom the word "affair" had a different meaning, was also there.

If you are lucky, you may see Holden (Edward Norton) singing to his beloved Skyler (Drew

Barrymore) near one of the fountains in front of the museum, in *Everyone Says I Love You*.

Remain on Fifth Avenue and turn right, walking north to 84th Street. At 84th Street, look across Fifth to see a path that leads into Central Park. This is the starting point for **Walking Tour 6: Central Park**, if you are to take it at this time. However, since **Walking Tour 6: Central Park** does not end at the place where it begins, you might want to take it at another time.

Assuming you are still with me, cross 84th and stop at the first building on the north side of the street. Walk to the door, just past the corner, up Fifth Avenue.

14. 1031 Fifth Avenue (Door Just North of 84th Street). As the cast of characters was introduced prior to the disaster looming beneath the waters of the Hudson River, a wealthy couple took their dog, Cooper, into Manhattan to visit a veterinarian who was located behind this door. As they left, they had no idea what was in store for them on their trip back home, in *Daylight*.

Continue north on Fifth Avenue stopping just before you get to 87th Street.

15. 1056 Fifth Avenue (at 87th Street). As part of their plan of revenge, Brenda, Elise and Annie had to break into the files of Brenda's "ex" Morty to get his phony books, in *The First Wives Club*. While Morty and girlfriend Shelly were kept busy by interior designer Duarte (Bronson Pinchot), the women did their digging.

However, Morty and Shelly came back too soon, and the first wives were forced to make their escape out a window and onto a window cleaning platform that was, coincidentally, parked outside Morty and Shelly's terrace.

Continue north up Fifth Avenue half a block until you are in front of 1067 Fifth Avenue.

16. 1067 Fifth Avenue (between 87ᵗʰ and 88ᵗʰ Streets). This building was home to wealthy Tom Mullen (Mel Gibson) and his wife Kate (Rene Russo), as well as their son Sean (Brawley Nolte), who was kidnapped while in Central Park (see **Walking Tour 6: Central Park**), in *Ransom*. As Tom sat sobbing on his terrace, the Guggenheim Museum, designed by Frank Lloyd Wright, was visible a short block to the north.

This building is also where Mrs. DaSilva, the supposed sister of Jimmy Dell (Steve Martin), lived. The gullible Joe Ross (Campbell Scott) dropped off a book ("Budge on Tennis") from Jimmy for his sister. Joe left the book with the doorman, but on a later visit learned the truth about Mrs. DaSilva, in *The Spanish Prisoner*.

Continue north until you are in front of the Guggenheim Museum.

17. 1071 Fifth Avenue. Guggenheim Museum. Responsible for the safety of the only witness in a murder case, Detective Mike Keegan (Tom Berenger) escorted the beautiful witness, Claire Gregory (Mimi Rogers), to a function at this museum, in *Someone to Watch Over Me*. Un-

fortunately, Detective Keegan, sidetracked by a chatty woman, lost sight of Claire, who, when she went to the ladies room, was threatened by the murder suspect, Joey Venza (Andreas Katsulas). Moments later, the two men had a confrontation out front.

———✦———

Continue north on Fifth until you reach 91st Street. Turn right on 91st.

18. 2 East 91st Street. National Design Museum. Unbeknownst to Jack Trainer (Harrison Ford), he and Tess McGill (Melanie Griffith) had not been invited to the wedding they were about to attend, given by Mr. Trask (Philip Bosco) for his daughter, in *Working Girl*. As Jack complained to Tess and wondered what she was up to, they walked along this fence and entered the building under this unique awning.

Although this building is actually a museum, in the movie *Arthur* it was suggested that the building was the home of Martha (Geraldine Fitzger-

ald), the wealthy matriarch of the well-connected Bach family.

———✦———

Continue past 2 East 91st and walk east until you are across from 7 East 91st.

19. 7 East 91st Street. This building was home to the lavish apartment that Steven and Emily Taylor called home, in *A Perfect Murder*. The tranquility of the surroundings was shattered by a break-in that forever changed their lives.

Return to Fifth Avenue and turn right, heading north until you reach 96th Street. Turn right on 96th and stop across from the door above a few stairs, just west of 9 East 96th Street.

20. 9 East 96th Street. After lunch with Alice, the unhappily married woman with whom he was having an affair, Joe, still invisible thanks to a magic potion, came here to eavesdrop on his ex-wife's therapy session. What he heard made him glad, but was not music to Alice's ears, in *Alice*.

Now comes the time for a decision. If you have seen *The Professional*, starring Jean Reno and Natalie Portman, then you may be up for a quick (5-minute) detour. If you choose to take the detour, continue here. If not, skip this next location and follow the directions to location 22.

For the detour continue east on 96th Street for two blocks to Park Avenue. Turn left on Park and walk north. Cross 96th Street and walk to the near corner of 97th Street. Note the building just to the left of the grocery on the corner, across 97th.

21. 71 East 97th Street. Leon (Jean Reno) led a simple life. He lived in this humble building, where he slept on the floor and cared for his houseplant. When asked, he provided "services" for Tony (Danny Aiello). But his life was changed forever when he rescued his young neighbor, Mathilda (Natalie Portman), whose entire family had been killed by a gang of rogue cops, led by the roguest of them all, Stansfield (Gary Oldman), in *The Professional*.

Fans of Star Wars may be interested to know that the young Natalie Portman from *The Professional* was the same one who went on to portray Princess Amidala in *Star Wars Episode I: The Phantom Menace*.

If you have taken the detour, head back south on Park Avenue, cross 96th Street and turn right, heading west to Madison Avenue. Cross to the far side of Madison and turn left. If you didn't take the detour, you are already on 96th Street and you should walk east to Madison and turn right. Walk south for 2 blocks, then turn to see the towering red brick facade of the castle across the street.

22. Madison Avenue (between 94th and 95th Streets). In *The Fisher King*, Jack Lukas (Jeff Bridges) had to get the Holy Grail for Perry (Robin Williams), in order to restore Perry to sanity and, possibly, to atone for having indirectly led to the death of Perry's wife three years before. The Holy Grail was believed to be in the possession of Langdon Carmichael, a reclusive billionaire, who purportedly lived in this "castle," which we can now see is nothing more than the front to a playground. In the movie, we get to see Jack

scale the outside of the "castle," to sneak in through one of the upper-level windows.

Continue south on Madison until you get to 93rd Street. Turn left on 93rd and stop in front of 55 East 93rd Street.

23. 55 East 93rd Street. Within this elegant looking building loomed a growing menace. A war was on, and Nazi spies were using this building for purposes of espionage. Despite the title of this documentary-style film, *The House on 92nd Street*, the building was actually located here, on 93rd Street. Poetic license wins again.

Return to Madison Avenue and turn left, going south on Madison until just before the corner of 90th Street.

24. 1261 Madison Avenue (at 90th Street). Having agreed to give the man who kidnapped his son $4,000,000 just to go away, Tom Mullen

and the kidnapper, Jimmy (Gary Sinise), came to the bank supposedly located in this building in order to transfer the money to Jimmy's account, in *Ransom*. Afterwards, a chase took place on the street behind you.

Continue south on Madison for two more blocks, until you reach 88th Street. Turn right on 88th, cross Madison and walk west to number Nineteen.

25. 19 East 88th Street. J.C. Wyatt (Diane Keaton) may not have had a perfect life, but she had a good life. Known as the Tiger Lady in business, she shared an apartment in this building with her equally successful boyfriend Steven (Harold Ramis). However, unlike J.C., he was not willing to give a young baby a chance to become a part of their lives, in *Baby Boom*.

Turn back and head east on 88th Street until you reach Park Avenue. Turn left on Park and walk north until just before 89th Street. Stop at 1088 Park Avenue.

26. 1088 Park Avenue. At a business meeting/luncheon to discuss the acquisition of art, Ouise Kittredge (Stockard Channing) stormed out on her friends, her colleagues and her husband Flanders (Donald Sutherland), in *Six Degrees of Separation*. Ouise and Flanders argued in front of this building, where she informed him that they no longer had all that much in common.

Tour 4

Continue to 89th Street and cross Park Avenue, heading east until you reach the Dalton School.

27. 108 East 89th Street. The Dalton School. In one of Woody Allen's older New York movies, 42-year-old Isaac (Woody Allen) was dating 17-year-old Tracy (Mariel Hemingway), in *Manhattan*. This is where Tracy was a high school student and where Isaac met her after school one day, got her a milkshake, and then broke off their relationship.

Continue east on 89th until you reach Lexington Avenue. Turn left on Lexington, going north until you reach 90th Street and are across from 1377 Lexington.

28. 1377 Lexington Avenue. Weitz, Weitz & Coleman Booksellers. Joe Ross was to deliver a book to the sister of Jimmy Dell, but the binding got damaged. Joe brought the "rare" volume here to be re-bound, only to find out that it was a relatively common edition, in *The Spanish Prisoner*.

Walk south on Lexington Avenue to 87th Street. Turn right on 87th and head west one block, to Park Avenue. Turn left on Park and stop in front of 1049 Park.

29. 1049 Park Avenue. Fans of the TV show "The Odd Couple" will recognize this building as the home of Oscar (Jack Klugman) and Felix (Tony Randall). In the show's familiar opening, as the two emerge from the building, Oscar throws down his cigar and Felix picks it up with the point of his umbrella. In the movie of the same name, the mismatched roommates lived in a different building (see **Walking Tour 3: The (Upper) Upper West Side**).

There is only one more stop on **Walking Tour 4: The Upper East Side**. To get there, continue south on Park until you get to 85th Street, then continue south the short distance to 1009 Park Avenue.

30. 1009 Park Avenue (at 85th Street). He thought he was the luckiest man alive, with a successful musical career and a young, beautiful wife, but Claude Eastman (Dudley Moore) had begun to suspect adultery. Claude and his possibly unfaithful wife, Daniella (Nastassja Kinski), lived here, in *Unfaithfully Yours*.

We have now come to the end of **Walking Tour 4: The Upper East Side**. As you are very close to the starting point for **Walking Tour 6: Central Park**, you may wish to take that tour now as well.

Walking Tour 5
THE FAR EAST

EAST
RIVE

E. 86TH ST.

UPTOWN

WEST
SIDE

EAST
SIDE

DOWNTOWN

LEXINGTON AVE.

THIRD AVE.

SECOND AVE.

FIRST AVE.

YORK AVE.

EAST END AVE.

E. 72ND ST.

E. 59TH ST.

ROOSEV

Walking Tour 5

THE FAR EAST

One of the more serene parts of Manhattan (at least further to the north), the Far East boasts the residence of New York City's Mayor, as well as the homes of thousands upon thousands of ordinary people. The name of this Walking Tour comes from the region's proximity to Manhattan's eastern boundary.

Walking Tour 5: The Far East begins at the corner of East End Avenue and 88th Street. If you choose to get to the starting point by public transportation, you may use any of the following subway (the closest subway stop is five long blocks away) or bus lines (although the following list is by no means exhaustive):

FROM THE NORTH
SUBWAYS
- **4, 5** or **6** southbound to 86th Street. Walk east on 86th to East End Avenue, then north on East End to 88th Street.

BUSES
- **M15** southbound on Second Avenue to 88th Street. Walk east on 88th to East End Avenue.
- **M31** southbound on York Avenue to 88th Street. Walk east on 88th to East End Avenue.

FROM THE SOUTH
SUBWAYS
- **4, 5** or **6** northbound to 86th Street. Walk east on 86th to East End Avenue, then north on East End to 88th Street.

BUSES

- **M15** northbound on First Avenue to 88th Street. Walk east on 88th to East End Avenue.

- **M31** northbound on York Avenue to 88th Street. Walk east on 88th to East End Avenue.

FROM THE WEST
BUSES

- **M31** eastbound on 57th Street, then north-bound on York Avenue, to 88th Street. Walk east on 88th to East End Avenue.

- **M66, M72** or **M79** eastbound to York Avenue. Transfer to **M31** northbound on York to 88th Street. Walk east on 88th to East End Avenue.

- **M86** eastbound to York Avenue. Walk east on 86th Street to East End Avenue, then north on East End to 88th Street.

- **M96** eastbound to Second Avenue. Transfer to **M15** southbound on Second to 88th Street. Walk east on 88th to East End Avenue.

The best place to begin **Walking Tour 5: The Far East**, is at the home of the person who presides over this great city, the Mayor. Walk to the northeast intersection of East End Avenue and 88th Street.

1. East End Avenue and 88th Street. Gracie Mansion. Much as the Mayor's "office" (City Hall) does (see **Walking Tour 13: Downtown and Financial District**), the Mayor's residence in real life also serves as the home of mayors in the movies. In *City Hall*, Mayor John Pappas (Al Pacino) presided over a dinner party to which his young deputy mayor Kevin Calhoun (John Cusack) arrived late. Other scenes between Pappas and Calhoun later on in the film also took place in the Mayor's residence.

Now turn and note the hospital located across the street.

2. 170 East End Avenue. Beth Israel Medical Center, North Division. The year was...well, that's not important. The month was March. The date, the 13th. Back then, this hospital was known as Doctor's Hospital. What happened there on that momentous day you ask? I was born. Consider yourself lucky, too. Had I not been born, you would be standing on this corner not knowing where to head next. But, luckily, I'm here to tell you.

———•–•———

Head west on 88th Street until you come to Second Avenue. At Second, look across the street.

3. 1703 Second Avenue (between 88th and 89th Streets). Elaine's. For over 30 years a food and drink institution for New York's literary crowd, Elaine's has found its way into several movies. In *Manhattan*, Isaac (Woody Allen), Tracy (Mariel Hemingway), Yale (Michael Murphy) and Emily (Anne Byrne) sat at a table here at the beginning of the movie and discussed the essence of life, art and courage. Political pundits may note that in this scene Isaac remarked as he lit a cigarette that while he smoked, he didn't inhale. Years later, a Presidential candidate from Arkansas was to make the same claim about another type of smoke.

In another film, *Night and the City*, lawyer /boxing promoter Mr. Fabian (Robert DeNiro) entered the restaurant and invited Regis Philbin and wife, Joy, who were peacefully enjoying a meal, to attend one of the boxing matches that Fabian hoped to promote.

———•–•———

Head south on Second Avenue until you get to the far side of 85th Street. Look to the high-rise apartment building on the southeast corner of 85th Street and Second Avenue.

4. 300 East 85th Street (at Second Avenue). Francis Fitzpatrick (Mike McGlone) had been having an affair with his brother's ex-girlfriend Heather (Cameron Diaz), in *She's the One*. When his brother Mickey (Ed Burns) told him how Heather had worked her way through college, Francis needed time to sort things out. Finally making his decision, Francis raced to this building and when Heather emerged, they talked as her stretch limousine waited at the curb.

Continue south on Second Avenue until you reach 75th Street. Turn left on 75th and head east until you are in front of 333 East 75th.

5. 333 East 75th Street. Lenny (Woody Allen) had tracked down the biological mother of his adopted son and had made an appointment to see her. The mother, Linda Ash (Mira Sorvino) was a hooker, but Lenny only wanted to talk, to learn all about her. Linda lived in this building and the two of them became good friends, in *Mighty Aphrodite*.

Retrace your steps on 75th Street to Second Avenue. Make a left on Second and head south until you reach 72nd Street. Cross 72nd, turn right and head west the short distance until you are in front of 242 East 72nd Street.

6. 242 East 72nd Street. In *Basketball Diaries*, Jim (Leonardo DiCaprio) paid two visits to this building. In the first, he and a friend were shown a great time by the sisters, Winkie (Cynthia Daniel) and Blinkie (Brittany Daniel). Later on, after he had gotten himself in trouble, he went back to see the two sisters. But this time they denied knowing him and their father kicked him out.

<hr>

Head back in the other direction. You should be walking east on 72nd Street. Stop when you reach York Avenue.

7. York Avenue and 72nd Street. Sotheby's.

Tom Logan (Robert Redford) and Laura J. Kelly (Debra Winger) were out to solve the murder of Sebastian Dierdon, a well-known artist. The murder had occurred years before, but now the artist's daughter Chelsea (Daryl Hannah) found herself implicated, and the two legal eagles decided to determine what really happened, in *Legal Eagles*. Tom and Laura interrupted Victor Taft (Terrence Stamp) during an auction being held here.

<hr>

Continue east on 72nd Street, all the way to the end. Stop outside the low-rise buildings on the left.

8. 535–541 East 72nd Street.

After running into Holly (Dianne Wiest), his former sister-in-law, Mickey Sachs (Woody Allen) spent some time with her, in *Hannah and Her Sisters*. Holly read Mickey her manuscript, which Mickey loved. Af-

terwards, they emerged from a doorway in this building and went to have something to eat.

Head away from the river, west, on 72nd Street, until you get back to First Avenue. Turn left and head south on First until you reach 68th Street. Turn right on 68th and walk west to 359 East 68th.

9. 359 East 68th Street. Spurned mistress Dolores (Anjelica Huston) having become a bit of a problem, Judah Rosenthal (Martin Landau) had decided to have something done about it. This building is where Dolores lived, and where she met her fate, courtesy of Judah's brother Jack (Jerry Orbach), in *Crimes and Misdemeanors*.

Return to First Avenue and make a right on First. In response to the famous Abbott and Costello question, "Who's on First?" you can now answer, truthfully, that you are. Walk south on First Avenue until you get to the corner of 63rd Street. Look across First to the building on the northeast corner (1152 First Avenue). The place has changed names, but in the movie *Cocktail*, this location was featured prominently.

10. First Avenue and 63rd Street. Northeast Corner. In *Cocktail*, Brian Flanagan (Tom

Cruise), after completing his military service, came to New York and tried unsuccessfully to find a job. He ventured into Wall Street (the finance world), Madison Avenue (advertising) and other fields, but his lack of education held him back. However, passing by the bar at this corner, he noticed a "Help Wanted" sign, went in and met Douglas Coughlin (Bryan Brown). From then on, somewhere inside, they "reigned as they poured."

Continue south on First until you reach 60th Street. Turn right on 60th and walk west the short distance until you are in front of Scores.

11. 333 East 60th Street. Scores. One of their own was about to be married, and the cops who populated a town known as Cop Land came here for a bachelor party. After watching one of them get sick beside a parked car across the street, Murray (Michael Rapaport) drove home, only to get into a whole lot of trouble on the George Washington Bridge, in *Cop Land*. Not long before the movie was filmed, Scores was the scene of a real murder that seemed straight out of a Hollywood script, one that involved revenge and allegations of ties to New York's underworld.

Return to First Avenue and turn right. Walk south to the south side of 59th Street. Turn right on 59th and walk west until you are across from 346 East 59th Street (the door is up a couple of steps, behind a tree).

12. 346 East 59th Street. After their misadventure in the Bronx, Sherman McCoy (Tom Hanks) and his mistress Maria (Melanie Griffith) ended up here, where Maria had an apartment, in *The Bonfire of the Vanities*.

You will notice that you are in the shadows of the 59th Street Bridge.

13. 59th Street Bridge (*aka* Queensboro Bridge). Besides being immortalized in the song "Feeling Groovy" by Simon and Garfunkel, the bridge has had its share of the cinematic spotlight. In *Manhattan*, Isaac and Mary (Diane Keaton) sat on a bench just south of the bridge, taking in its splendor.

In *Home Alone 2: Lost in New York*, Kevin McAllister (Macaulay Culkin) took a cab from the airport and entered Manhattan this way, as have characters in many other movies.

Fans of the television show "Taxi" might be interested to know (if they don't already) that in the opening sequence of the show, a taxicab is also shown crossing this bridge into Manhattan.

Walk west on 59th Street (away from First Avenue). As you walk, keep looking up and to the right to see if the Roosevelt Island Tram comes into view. If not, continue until you reach Second Avenue, where you will see the Tram's Manhattan terminal, if not the Tram itself, one block to the north.

14. Roosevelt Island Tram. A band of terrorists, led by Rutger Hauer, had taken hostages aboard the Tram as it dangled beside the bridge, high over the East River. In a daring rescue, as per

the terrorists' instructions, Detective DaSilva (Sylvester Stallone) was lowered from a helicopter to receive one of the hostages, an infant the terrorists released to show they were not monsters, in *Nighthawks*.

Cross to the west side of Second Avenue. Turn right and walk north on Second to 60th Street. Make a left on 60th and walk west until you are across from Serendipity 3.

15. 225 East 60th Street. Serendipity 3. Taking a pause during their extremely hectic day in *One Fine Day*, Melanie Parker (Michelle Pfeiffer) took son Sammy (Alex D. Linz) and Maggie (Mae Whitman), the daughter of flirtatious nemesis Jack Taylor (George Clooney), for ice cream at this East Side favorite.

Continue west on 60th Street until you reach Lexington Avenue. Turn right on Lexington and stop in front of Bloomingdale's.

16. Lexington Avenue (between 60th and 61st Streets). Bloomingdale's. Fed up with life in the Soviet Union, Vladimir (Robin Williams), a musician with a Russian circus, decided to defect. He did so while the circus was on a last-minute shopping trip at Bloomingdale's, before heading back to Moscow, in *Moscow on the Hudson*.

Fans of the television show "Friends" will remember that Rachel (Jennifer Aniston) for a while worked here at Bloomingdale's.

<hr />

Continue north on Lexington until you reach 63rd Street. Turn right on 63rd.

17. 140 East 63rd Street (at Lexington Avenue). Barbizon Hotel.

With his days of boxing behind him, the pudgy Jake LaMotta (Robert DeNiro), at the end of *Raging Bull*, sat in his dressing room in this hotel, where he was the featured performer in "An Evening With Jake LaMotta." The evening would feature the works of Paddy Chayefsky, Rod Serling, Shakespeare, Budd Schulberg and Tennessee Williams. In a poignant scene, it showed that nothing lasts forever.

<hr />

Continue east on 63rd Street to Third Avenue. Make a left on Third, head north and make a right on 66th Street. Walk east on 66th (on the curb in the middle of the block—the stone wall should be on your right) until halfway down the block.

18. East 66th Street between Third and Second Avenues.

In *Annie Hall*, Alvie Singer (Woody Allen) was talking with close friend Rob (Tony Roberts) about life, anti-semitism and Annie Hall (Diane Keaton). As they walked, Alvie revealed the anti-semitic remark someone had made at the office. They had been talking about lunch, and someone asked Alvie if he had eaten lunch. But the man's question did not come across to Alvie as "Did you?" It came across as "Di-jew?" Best friend Rob could only try to placate his paranoid friend as they walked along this streeet.

<hr />

Woody Allen also used this street in a later and darker film. In *Crimes and Misdemeanors*, Judah

Rosenthal had asked his brother Jack to help him with his "situation" involving spurned mistress Dolores. Jack did just that. In a scene more likely to be found in an old Hitchcock film than one by Woody Allen, Dolores was followed down this street one evening by a mysterious man. Later that night, Judah learned that he had nothing to fear from the woman ever again.

Continue east to Second Avenue. Note the movie theatre across the street.

19. 1254 Second Avenue (at 66th Street). Beekman Theatre. Certain that his wife Daniella (Nastassja Kinski) was having an affair, symphony conductor Claude Eastman (Dudley Moore) followed her into this theatre and searched for her in the dark, in *Unfaithfully Yours*. Seeing an affectionate couple several rows up, Claude confronted them. He found himself embarrassed and, a short time later, in the custody of the police.

You have now reached the end of **Walking Tour 5: The Far East**. From here, it is not far to the starting points for **Walking Tour 1: 57th Street Shopper's Delight** or **Walking Tour 4: The Upper East Side**. It would make sense to strike while the iron is hot.

Walking Tour 6
CENTRAL PARK

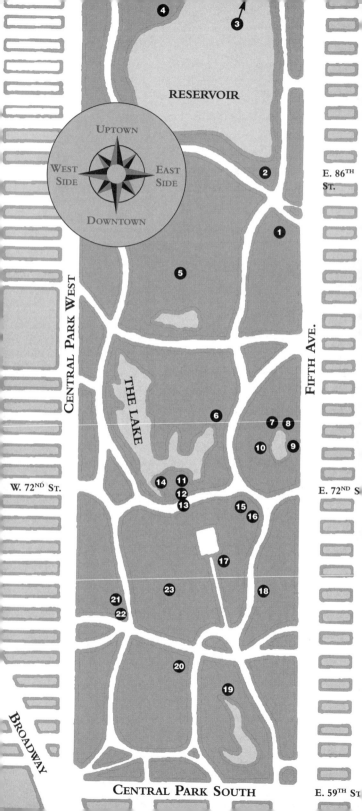

Walking Tour 6
CENTRAL PARK

A beautiful example of the marriage of nature and design, Central Park is for visitors one of the most unexpected treasures of New York. Most people from elsewhere only hear horror stories about this New York City gem and believe it to be one of the most dangerous places on earth, but nothing could be further from the truth. Hopefully, a brief trip through Central Park should convince the TourWalker of its beauty and abundance of pleasures.

Walking Tour 6: Central Park begins at the corner of Fifth Avenue and 84th Street. If you choose to get to the starting point by public transportation, you may use any of the following subway or bus lines (although the following list is by no means exhaustive):

FROM THE NORTH
SUBWAYS
- **4, 5** or **6** southbound to 86th Street. Walk west on 86th to Fifth Avenue, then south on Fifth to 84th Street.

BUSES
- **M1, M2, M3** or **M4** southbound on Fifth Avenue to 84th Street.
- **M101, M102** or **M103** southbound on Lexington Avenue to 84th Street. Walk west on 84th to Fifth Avenue.

FROM THE SOUTH
SUBWAYS

- **4, 5** or **6** northbound to 86th Street. Walk west on 86th to Fifth Avenue, then south on Fifth to 84th Street.

BUSES

- **M1, M2, M3** or **M4** northbound on Madison Avenue to 84th Street. Walk west on 84th to Fifth Avenue.

- **M101, M102** or **M103** northbound on Third Avenue to 84th Street. Walk west on 84th to Fifth Avenue.

FROM THE EAST
BUSES

- **M31, M57, M66, M72** or **M79** westbound to Madison Avenue. Transfer to **M1, M2, M3** or **M4** northbound on Madison to 84th Street. Walk west on 84th to Fifth Avenue.

- **M86** westbound on 86th Street to Fifth Avenue. Walk south on Fifth to 84th Street.

- **M96** westbound to Fifth Avenue. Transfer to **M1, M2, M3** or **M4** southbound on Fifth to 84th Street.

FROM THE WEST
BUSES

- **M66** or **M72** eastbound to Madison Avenue. Transfer to **M1, M2, M3** or **M4** northbound on Madison to 84th Street. Walk west on 84th to Fifth Avenue.

- **M79** eastbound to Fifth Avenue. Walk north on Fifth to 84th Street.

- **M86** eastbound to Fifth Avenue and 84th Street.

- **M96** eastbound to Fifth Avenue. Transfer to **M1, M2, M3** or **M4** southbound on Fifth to 84th Street.

Beginning at the southwest corner of Fifth Avenue and 84th Street (the northern corner of the Metropolitan Museum of Art), walk west and then bear left on the path leading into Central Park. As you enter the park, note the enormous wall of glass, the Egyptian Pavilion, on your left.

1. Metropolitan Museum of Art. Egyptian Pavilion. Harry Burns (Billy Crystal) and Sally Albright (Meg Ryan) had become good friends, in *When Harry Met Sally . . . .* One sunny afternoon, they wandered through this pavilion, with Harry giving Sally amusing diction lessons, during which he asked Sally if she would like to see a movie that night. Much to his dismay, he learned that Sally had a date. From that point forward, they realized their interest in each other might be more than just as friends.

Continue along the path (keeping the Museum on your left) until you reach the roadway (Park Drive East). Cross the roadway to the other side, turn right and walk north a short distance until you see the path on the left, leading to the Reservoir. Climb the steps to the Reservoir. Avoid the runners as they whoosh by.

2. Reservoir. South Gate House. Although he was not sure how, Babe (Dustin Hoffman) found himself involved in matters of international intrigue. In a final scene here, in *Marathon Man,*

Babe had led Szell (Sir Laurence Olivier) into this building in a final effort to find out "if it's safe."

While you are welcome to circle the Reservoir (it is roughly 1.6 miles around), it is not necessary to do so for purposes of **Walking Tour 6: Central Park.** There are a few movie scenes that have been filmed around the Reservoir, but I will summarize them right here, so you don't have to do the walking. All you have to do is climb the steps and glimpse the reservoir from a safe vantage point (avoid the runners).

3. Reservoir. Northeastern Side, east of North Building. Wrestling with many demons —among them young upstart Kevin Lomax (Keanu Reeves), who may have been after his job as head of the law firm—Eddie Barzoom (Jeffrey Jones) was out for a run, in *The Devil's Advocate.* It would be his last run, as Eddie was pursued by demonic beings who assumed the forms of New York's homeless before beating him to death just off the Reservoir path.

4. Reservoir. Northwestern tip. Running Track. Depressed about the meaning of life, and pondering the thoughts of such great thinkers as Socrates, Nietzsche and Freud (but not heeding the warning to stay off the track itself), Mickey Sachs (Woody Allen) walked north along the west side of the Reservoir, in *Hannah and Her Sisters.* In the movie, the Citicorp Building was clearly visible in the background.

Along the same stretch of the Reservoir, Patrick (Mike McGlone) confronted Susan (Shari Albert), who had jilted him just before he could break off his relationship with her, in *The Brothers McMullen.*

Head back down the steps from the Reservoir,

turn right, walk the short distance south, and cross back to the Museum side of Park Drive East. Turn right and walk south on the path that runs parallel to the drive. At the point where the path comes closest to the road, you will see the Obelisk (a tall, needle-like structure) across the road on the right. Continue south on the path and when you are directly across from the Obelisk, continue on the path as it slopes down. At the base of the path, turn right and cross under the road through Greywacke Arch. When you emerge, you will be heading west, toward the Great Lawn. Walk straight until you reach the Great Lawn, turn left and walk until the Castle is clearly in view.

5. Path to north of Belvedere Castle. Learning that the responsibility of caring for an infant also came with incredible benefits, perennial bachelors Jack (Ted Danson), Michael (Steve

Guttenberg) and Peter (Tom Selleck) threw frisbees and collected women's phone numbers one pleasant afternoon along this spot, in *Three Men and a Baby*.

Turn left and follow the path closest to the water (Turtle Pond). After you pass the statue of King Jagiello, make a left on the path that slopes upward. The path will reconnect with Park Drive East. At the road, turn right and head south along the side of the road (on the grass, where possible) until you reach the Loeb Boathouse Cafe (around 74th Street).

6. Loeb Boathouse Cafe. Park Drive East at 74th Street. Sally Albright was newly single, which she somehow let slip to her friend Marie

(Carrie Fisher) over lunch at an outdoor table at this restaurant, in *When Harry Met Sally....* Happy to help, Marie pulled out her rolodex and looked to see who might prove a worthy set-up for Sally.

At the Loeb Boathouse sign, cross Park Drive East and head east toward the building with the green roof (with luck, you may see miniature sailboats floating on the water). Walk down the path until you get to the pond. Turn left and walk along the pond until you are in front of the Alice in Wonderland statue (it's referred to as the Margarita Delacorte Memorial).

7. Sailboat Pond. Alice in Wonderland statue. After inviting her so-called boyfriend for a birthday dinner with her and her mother Hannah (Lauren Bacall), Rose (Barbra Streisand) strolled with Greg (Jeff Bridges) past this statue, in *The Mirror Has Two Faces*.

Realizing that their relationship may have reached a crossroads, Lisa (Brooke Adams) and

Phillip (Ben Masters) sat in front of this statue, discussing their future, in *Key Exchange*.

Just east of the statue turn toward the pond.

8. Sailboat Pond. From North East Corner. Sitting on a bench with this view before them, Nina (Jennifer Aniston) told her roommate and best friend (and the real though not realistic object of her affections), George (Paul Rudd), that she was pregnant, in *The Object of My Affections*.

Visible in the distance is a small building across the way. Fearing that he was being followed, Paul (George Peppard) walked along this pond and headed toward that small building, hoping to draw his pursuer (Buddy Ebsen) out, in *Breakfast at Tiffany's*.

Walk a little further until you are in front of the building with the green roof at the east end of the sailboat pond.

9. Central Park. Alice and Edward Kerbs Memorial Building. Knowing that something had gone wrong with his assignment and sensing that something sinister was taking place with him as the next victim, Rollie Tyler (Bryan Brown) hid in this building until his assistant Andy (Martha Gehman) showed up with his special ef-

fects bag, in *F/X*. A man had followed Andy, and Rollie, sensing his only opportunity, pushed the man in the water and fled into the anonymity of Central Park.

———◆—◆———

Continue around the pond to the other side and start up the path to the left of the statue of Hans Christian Andersen, pausing briefly near the statue.

10. Central Park. Hans Christian Andersen statue. Old friends Midge (Ossie Davis) and Nat (Walter Matthau) spent a good deal of their free

time in Central Park and on at least one occasion, sat in front of the statue of this famed storyteller, in *I'm Not Rappaport*.

———◆—◆———

Continue along the path, cross back to the Boathouse Cafe and follow the path along the left side of the water, past the line of docked row-boats. Continue along the path (bear right as the path forks) until you reach Bethesda Fountain.

11. Bethesda Fountain. If you like, you can circle around the Fountain and approach it from the other side (the west). If you do, you will be following in the footsteps of Georges (Gerard Depardieu) and Bronte (Andie MacDowell) as they

Tour 6

wandered around, in *Green Card*, getting to know one another before taking the test to prove they were, in fact, married.

In another film, the serene beauty of this fountain was spoiled, first by the congestion of the 10th Annual New York City Junior Science Fair, and second, by the kidnapping of young Sean Mullen (Brawley Nolte) at that fair, in *Ransom*. While his wife Kate (Rene Russo), the chairwoman of the science fair, presided over the proceedings, airline executive Tom Mullen (Mel Gibson) lost sight of his son for only an instant. But that was all it took.

In another film, *Deconstructing Harry*, in one of the film's stories within the story, a crew was filming a scene when they discovered that the star, Mel (Robin Williams), was literally out-of-focus, while the rest of the actors were clear.

While filming scenes for his documentary around the fountain, Pete (Jack Lemmon) made an incredible discovery: Gladys Glover (Judy Holliday), in *It Should Happen to You*.

Head south from the Fountain toward the archways on your right.

12. Bethesda Fountain. North of 72nd Street Transverse. Their one long yet fine day almost over, Melanie Parker (Michelle Pfeiffer) and Jack

Taylor (George Clooney) raced through Central Park to get the kids to a soccer game, in *One Fine Day*. They emerged from the staircase under this archway and onto the Bethesda Fountain Plaza, and took a few moments to splash joyfully in the puddles before heading over to the playing field.

As you stand here, be careful. If you see Kevin McAllister (Macaulay Culkin) come running at the fountain toward you, you may have to step out of his way very quickly. Although Kevin is small, he will be followed closely by those two evil meanies, Marv (Daniel Stern) and Harry (Joe Pesci), in hot pursuit, in *Home Alone 2: Lost in New York*.

Walk through the archway and up the first level of stairs, until you see the men's room on the right.

13. Men's Room. Staircase leading to Bethesda Fountain.

Suspicious of Jimmy Dell (Steve Martin), with whom Joe (Campbell Scott) was to have a meeting at the Carousel, Joe first met a supposed federal agent (Ed O'Neill) in this men's room, in *The Spanish Prisoner*. Remember, however, that this book is about movie exteriors. I do not know whether the meeting was actually filmed in this men's room, and do not suggest that you find out unless you have to.

Walk up the steps and turn right at the top. Make another right and walk to the 72nd Street Transverse. Carefully cross the Transverse to the north side, where you'll get a great view of Bethesda Fountain. Turn left and walk west (about 100 yards) until you come to the first road leading to the right. Head up that road until you come to the circular road surrounding a small fountain.

14. Fountain off 72nd Street Transverse. Jack Jericho (Robert Downey, Jr.) had picked up Randy Jensen (Molly Ringwald) one morning before work, in *The Pick-Up Artist*. In Jack's car, which he managed to park next to this fountain, the two of them engaged without interruption in a little early morning delight.

Return to the 72nd Street Transverse and head left, back toward the steps leading to Bethesda Fountain. When you reach the top of the steps, carefully cross the Transverse and head south toward the bandshell.

15. Central Park Bandshell. South of 72nd Street Transverse. A well-known musical venue in its own right, the bandshell has appeared in several movies. In *Mighty Aphrodite*, Lenny (Woody Allen) decided to set up Linda (Mira Sorvino), the biological mother of his adopted son, on a blind date with Kevin (Michael Rapaport). They met in front of the bandshell.

Trying to find ways to stop being a lonely guy, Larry (Steve Martin) rented a dog and sat with the dog and a lonely friend, Warren (Charles Grodin), on the benches next to the bandshell, in *The Lonely Guy*. Unfortunately, the move was a bust. Larry met no one and was given a ticket because the dog pooped on the pathway.

In *Breakfast at Tiffany's*, Paul sat near the bandshell and talked to Fred (Buddy Ebsen), the man who had been following him. Fred, the husband of the beautiful Holly Golightly (Audrey Hepburn), wanted Paul's help to get her back, not knowing that Paul was falling in love with Holly, too.

Unlike the films where the characters met or sat near the bandshell, in *I'm Not Rappaport*, adversarial companions Nat and Midge performed an old soft shoe on the stage for the benefit of a very small audience.

As you face the bandshell, note the stairs leading directly behind the bandshell, and climb them.

16. Walkway behind Bandshell. As Ted Kramer (Dustin Hoffman) tried to break the news to his son Billy (Justin Henry) that Billy had to go live with his mother, they walked along here, in *Kramer vs. Kramer*.

Descend the staircase and return to the front of the bandshell. Head south along the Mall (a wide thoroughfare with benches on both sides).

17. The Mall. You may have to step around Ted and Billy, who have just spotted Billy's mom, Joanna (Meryl Streep), in *Kramer vs. Kramer*. In a memorable scene, Ted gives his son a little pep talk before sending him back to his mom, who won the custody battle between the Kramers.

Tour 6

Continue walking in the same direction. Where the Mall lets out, you will see a few statues. At the statue of Shakespeare (on your left), walk to the road. You will see two sets of traffic lights. Cross the road and turn left on the path that starts on the other side of the traffic lights. The path runs to the north and is parallel to the road. Stay on the path as it slopes down until you come to the Statue of Balto (a big dog).

18. Statue of Balto. East of Park Drive East.

Not only is Balto the subject of the animated movie *Balto*, but the statue itself was shown in *Six Degrees of Separation*. Flanders (Donald Sutherland) and Ouise (Stockard Channing) were having a guest over for dinner, when their hospitality was tested by a mysterious visitor, Paul (Will Smith), who appeared to be hurt. Paul revealed that he was standing in Central Park, looking at the statue of Balto (and wondering what a statue commemorating a dog from Alaska was doing in the middle of Central Park), when he was mugged. In a later scene, Paul sat by the statue with a young couple he befriended.

Retrace your steps up the path. At the second set of traffic lights (not the set you crossed at before), cross to the path that runs alongside the road. You should be on the opposite side of the road from the statues. Follow the curve of the road as it winds left. In a couple of minutes, you should see a small building up the hill on the left. This is the Chess & Checkers House (across the road from the Carousel). Walk up the path toward the building, along the benches and descend the back stairs. Turn right at the bottom and follow the path to Wollman Rink.

19. Park Drive. Wollman Rink. While revelers whizzed by on their skates, Marv and Harry plot-

ted their next caper, unaware that Kevin McAllister was near, in *Home Alone 2: Lost in New York*.

Newly reinstated to the police department and assigned to the case of a serial killer terrorizing New York, Nick Starkey (Kevin Kline) followed the Mayor's daughter Bernadette (Mary Elizabeth Mastrantonio) from her friend's funeral to this rink, where he initiated contact, in *The January Man*.

Leave Wollman Rink and head west. Walk through Driprock Arch. Make a right on the first path on which you can make a right and follow the path to the Carousel.

20. Park Drive. Carousel. Bright yet gullible Joe was out to make sure he got what was coming to him for having invented "the Process" in *The Spanish Prisoner*. As instructed by the F.B.I., Joe waited at this Carousel for Jimmy Dell, or Jimmy's contact, to arrive. It was a long wait.

Usually intended for children, the Carousel was ridden by old codgers Midge and Nat while The Cowboy (Craig T. Nelson) talked on his cell phone nearby, in *I'm Not Rappaport*.

Presumably they rode the ponies at a different time than Max Bialystock (Zero Mostel) and Leo Bloom (Gene Wilder), who enjoyed the

Carousel during an extended lunch break, in *The Producers*.

Walk up the hill past the Carousel (the Playmates Arch should be on your right) and turn left at the road. As the road curves to the right, turn left up the path (uphill). The fenced-in area known as Sheep Meadow should be on your right and the Carousel should be on your left. Follow the winding path west until you are across from Tavern on the Green. Carefully cross Park Drive, turn right and walk north the short distance to the restaurant's entrance.

21. Tavern on the Green. Entrance. Having just met with Gordon Gecko (Michael Douglas) in Central Park on an appropriately rainy day, in *Wall Street*, the once-promising Bud Fox (Charlie Sheen) walked toward the entrance to Tavern on the Green and into a restroom within. There, federal agents helped remove the tape recorder from his body and checked the tape. It was clear that Gordon's high-flying days were numbered.

A familiar eatery and a very popular one at that, Tavern on the Green is also where Sheldon (Woody Allen) had to endure a lunch with his overbearing mother and a few other people in the "Oedipus Wrecks" segment of *New York Stories*. The whole time, Mom complained about having to sit outside—something most people request during nice weather.

The restaurant is also where Ellen (Annabella Sciorra) had lunch with Lucy (Christine Baranski), and told her that she had taken an apartment in the city two days a week in which to do her painting, in *The Night We Never Met*. The building where that apartment is can be seen on **Walking Tour 10: The Village**.

Turn left from the entrance and walk south the

short distance until you are outside Tavern on the Green's dining patio.

22. Tavern on the Green. Dining Patio. Louis Tully (Rick Moranis) had his party interrupted by a beast, in *Ghostbusters*. The beast chased Louis out of his building (see **Walking Tour 2: The (Lower) Upper West Side**) and into Central Park. Moments later, as diners enjoyed their meals, Louis was attacked by the beast outside the picture windows behind the dining patio.

Continue south along Park Drive. Take a last look at the grass on your left.

23. Central Park. Grass. If I mention where it was actually filmed, everyone might end up doing it, but just imagine lying somewhere in the park, admiring the starlit night sky, stark naked. That is what Perry (Robin Williams) and Jack (Jeff Bridges) did in *The Fisher King*. In this park. At night. Somewhere.

During the less isolated daylight hours, somewhere on the lawn, two ants, Z (voice of Woody Allen) and Princess Bala (voice of Sharon Stone) made their way to a veritable oasis a long distance (to ants, anyway) from their home, somewhere out on the Central Park grass, in *Antz*.

You have reached the end of **Walking Tour 6: Central Park**. If you continue south until you come to the Park's exit at Columbus Circle, you will emerge at the starting point for **Walking Tour 2: The (Lower) Upper West Side**. Be my guest.

Walking Tour 7
MIDTOWN

THE MUSIC HALL

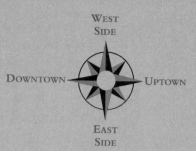

AVE. AMERICAS

FIFTH AVE.

MADISON AVE.

PARK AVE.

LEXINGTON AVE.

THIRD AVE.

SECOND AVE.

FIRST AVE.

Walking Tour 7
MIDTOWN

With a skyline like no other city on earth, Midtown Manhattan appears sterile and anonymous to some, but that image is just a facade. To those who look closely, Midtown harbors the lifeblood of the city, as well as numerous locations that have won the affections of location scouts and moviegoers alike.

Walking Tour 7: Midtown begins at the northwest corner of Park Avenue and 39th Street. If you choose to get to the starting point by public transportation, you may use any of the following subway or bus lines (although the following list is by no means exhaustive):

FROM THE NORTH
SUBWAYS
- **4, 5** or **6** southbound to 42nd Street/Grand Central Station. Walk south on Park Avenue to 39th Street.

BUSES
- **M1** southbound on Fifth Avenue, then Park Avenue, to 39th Street.

- **M2, M3** or **M4** southbound on Fifth Avenue to 39th Street. Walk east on 39th to Park Avenue.

- **M101, M102** or **M103** southbound on Lexington Avenue to 39th Street. Walk west on 39th to Park Avenue.

FROM THE SOUTH
SUBWAYS

- **1, 2, 3, 9, N** or **R** northbound to 42nd Street/Times Square. Transfer to **7** or **42nd Street Shuttle** eastbound to Grand Central Station. Walk south on Park Avenue to 39th Street.

- **4, 5** or **6** northbound to 42nd Street/Grand Central Station. Walk south on Park Avenue to 39th Street.

BUSES

- **M1** northbound on Park Avenue South, then Park Avenue, to 39th Street.

- **M2** or **M3** northbound on Park Avenue South, then Madison Avenue, to 39th Street. Walk east on 39th to Park Avenue.

- **M101, M102** or **M103** northbound on Third Avenue to 39th Street. Walk west on 39th to Park Avenue.

FROM THE EAST
BUSES

- **M42** or **M104** westbound on 42nd Street to Park Avenue. Walk south on Park to 39th Street.

FROM THE WEST
SUBWAYS

- **1, 2, 3** or **9** southbound to 42nd Street/Times Square. Transfer to **7** or **42nd Street Shuttle**.

- **7** or **42nd Street Shuttle** eastbound from Times Square to Grand Central Station. Walk south on Park Avenue to 39th Street.

BUSES

- **M16** or **M34** eastbound on 34th Street to Park Avenue. Walk north on Park to 39th Street.

- **M42** eastbound on 42nd Street to Park Avenue. Walk south on Park to 39th Street.

- **M104** southbound on Broadway, then east-bound on 42nd Street, to Park Avenue. Walk south on Park to 39th Street.

However you choose to get to Park Avenue and 39th Street, when you get there, walk to the northwest corner. You should see the grand façade of Grand Central Terminal and the MetLife Building staring down at you a couple of blocks to the north. Walk north half a block and turn toward the left. You should be in front of 90 Park Avenue.

1. 90 Park Avenue (between 39th and 40th Streets). New York City cop Leo McCarthy (Brian Dennehy) knew something was wrong. There was a dead federal agent, a borrowed social security number, and the agent's boss, Colonel Mason (Mason Adams) didn't seem curious to know how the man died. In *F/X*, Leo paid Colonel Mason a visit in this building to try and get some answers.

Look directly across Park Avenue to the large building on the east side of the street.

2. 99 Park Avenue. By night, Alice (Chloë Sevigny) and Charlotte (Kate Beckinsale) tripped the light fantastic at the hottest disco in town. By day, they trudged away as low-level workers in the publishing industry in this building, in *The Last Days of Disco*.

Continue north, to the near corner of Park Avenue, at 40th Street, and look diagonally across the street.

3. 101 Park Avenue. This large tower is one of those buildings that has found its way into numerous films over the years. In *Brewster's Millions*, baseball player Monty Brewster (Richard Pryor) stood to inherit a great deal of money ($300 million) if he could spend a much smaller sum ($30 million) in a month, with nothing to show for it. To get the details, he and a few others, including teammate Spike Nolan (John Candy), headed into this building to meet with the lawyers who had summoned him.

Similarly, in *The Fisher King*, when Jack Lukas (Jeff Bridges) decided he was ready to get back to work as a radio talk show host, he and his agent Lou (David Hyde Pierce) headed into this building to discuss such a step. Although Jack was confronted outside the building by the colorful cross-dressing character played by Michael Jeter, he initially ignored his conscience and pretended he didn't know the man.

In yet another film, Brantley Foster (Michael J. Fox), fresh off the farm, thought he would work here, in *The Secret of My Success*. His success would have to start somewhere else, however, because on his first day at work, he learned that most of the company's work force had been let go, the result of a hostile takeover.

Lastly, Alice (Mia Farrow) came here to visit her friend Nancy Brill (Cybill Shepherd) to toss around some ideas for a television series, in *Alice*.

Before crossing 40th Street, note the ramp intersecting 40th and Park.

4. 40th Street and Park Avenue (Traffic Ramp). Picking a bad day to try and get to the airport (thanks to the 50th-year celebration of the United Nations), West Coast resident Max (Wesley Snipes) sat fuming in the back seat of the taxi stalled at the foot of this ramp. Finally realizing he wasn't going anywhere, at least at that time, Max exited the cab and ended up in the arms of Karen (Nastassja Kinski), in *One Night Stand*.

Before taking another step, note the grand MetLife Building, just ahead on Park.

5. 200 Park Avenue. The MetLife Building. It looks okay now, but if you saw 1998's *Godzilla*, you may remember that as a result of the monster's visit to Manhattan, there was a gaping hole through the building, from one side to the other.

Continue north on Park Avenue and stop at the corner of 41st Street. The next location is on the northwest corner of the intersection.

6. 120 Park Avenue (at 41st Street). Pulling off a clever bank heist, Grimm (Bill Murray), dressed as a clown, entered this building and emerged a very rich man. All he had to do was get to the airport, in *Quick Change*.

Continue up Park Avenue until you reach 42nd Street. The grand entrance to famed Grand Central Station should loom before you. Be patient. We will work our way inside in due time. But first, turn right and walk the short distance until you are in front of 110 East 42nd Street.

7. 110 East 42nd Street. Always excited to accompany his "stern" father into the city, a young

Howard Stern (Bobby Borrello) followed his father Ben (Richard Portnow) into this building, where the elder Mr. Stern worked as a radio engineer, in Howard Stern's semi-autobiographical film, *Private Parts*.

Head back the other way on 42nd Street and walk west until you are in front of 60 East 42nd Street.

8. 60 East 42nd Street. The Lincoln Building.

Jack Taylor (George Clooney) was a successful reporter for the *Daily News*, whose offices were located in this building, in the romantic comedy *One Fine Day*.

Continue west on 42nd Street until you reach the corner of Fifth Avenue. Turn left at the corner and walk south a block until you are right across from the New York Public Library, another beautiful New York City landmark.

9. Fifth Avenue and 40th-42nd Streets. New York Public Library.

In *Ghostbusters*, Ray Stantz (Dan Aykroyd), Peter Venkman (Bill Murray) and Egon Spengler (Harold Ramis) had just seen their funding terminated and themselves removed from Columbia University (see **Walking Tour 3: The (Upper) Upper West Side**). But after an apparition in the image of a spinster librarian had been found in the lower levels of this building, the ghostbusters were called in, had an encounter with the none-too-friendly ghost and came running out the front doors of the library and down these stairs.

Return to 42nd Street and turn left, crossing Fifth Avenue. Continue walking west until you come to the first entrance to Bryant Park, just past the Library. If it's daylight and the park is open, enter the park and turn right along the first pathway, walking parallel to 42nd Street. If not, you can walk alongside the park and peek in from the street.

10. Bryant Park. 42nd Street between Fifth and Sixth Avenues. After getting fired from his job as a fact-checker for a magazine, Jamie Conway (Michael J. Fox) walked along this path and sat on a bench, where he was approached by one of the park's more colorful characters (William Hickey), in *Bright Lights, Big City*. Jamie was offered the choice between a ferret and cocaine. As a subsequent scene reveals, at the very least, he purchased the ferret.

Along this path you might also find former Wall Street whiz-kid Lewis (Christian Slater) and the object of his affections, Lisa (Mary Stuart Masterson), strolling during their day-long date, in *Bed of Roses*.

———◆———

Keep walking a bit, then turn and notice the fountain toward the western entrance to Bryant Park.

11. Bryant Park. Fountain. If you look closely, you might be able to see Larry (Woody Allen) meet up with his wife Carol (Diane Keaton) alongside the fountain, in *Manhattan Murder Mys-*

tery. Suspicious that their neighbor may have killed his wife, Carol had just broken into his apartment to snoop around. Always the voice of reason, Larry complained that Carol had done what's known in legal circles as "breaking and entering," but Carol maintained that she did as well as a private eye would have done.

Add a few thousand screaming fans to this small park and you've got a full-fledged celebra-

tion. That's what Howard Stern did at the end of *Private Parts*.

—————

Exit the park on 42nd Street and continue west to Sixth Avenue (Avenue of the Americas). Turn right on Sixth and walk north until you reach 44th Street. Turn right on 44th and head east until you are across from The Algonquin.

12. 59 West 44th Street. The Algonquin. During their heyday, from here they reigned supreme, their words piercing and illuminating the literary scene of the 1930s. Holding court at the legendary Algonquin Round Table were Alexander Woollcott, George S. Kaufman, Franklin P. Adams, Robert Benchley and Dorothy Parker, among others, and they were brought to life in *Mrs. Parker and the Vicious Circle*.

—————

Continue east until you are across from 37 West 44th Street.

13. 37 West 44th Street. This beautiful building, with its windows that seem to suggest a work by Salvador Dali, was an architectural site pointed out to Holly (Dianne Wiest) and April (Carrie Fisher) by David (Sam Waterston) in his tour, in *Hannah and Her Sisters*. Of course, while he was showing the catering partners his favorite locations, the women were focusing more on which of the two of them David was more interested in.

It is now time to take a look inside Grand Central Station. Continue east on 44th Street until you can't walk east anymore. You should be standing on Vanderbilt Avenue at the foot of the MetLife Building. Walk to the right and enter Grand Central Station through the Vanderbilt Avenue entrance.

14. Grand Central Station. Main Room. Imagine if you can the lights dimming, orchestral music playing and the frenzied commuters slowing down long enough to pair off and spend a few priceless moments waltzing. That is just what Perry (Robin Williams) did, in *The Fisher King*. As he followed his beloved Lydia (Amanda Plummer) through the rush-hour throng, everyone

began to waltz, in one of the most magical moments captured on film in recent decades.

You could also imagine, perhaps with more difficulty, the relative serenity of the scene below where you stand being shattered by a bombardment of asteriods, as it was in *Armageddon*.

Descend the staircase and find your way to the clock above the information booth in the center of the space. The best time here is during the day, when the sunlight streaks through the fabulous windows on every side. If possible, avoid the rush hours (8:00 to 10:00 A.M. and 4:00 to 7:00 P.M.). Otherwise, you won't get a great view of the different locations, and you might get trampled.

Unfortunately, this room has not always provided memories as wonderful as those in *The Fisher King*. In *Midnight Run*, bounty hunter Jack Walsh (Robert DeNiro) had learned that "the Duke" (Charles Grodin), the fugitive he was supposed to bring back to Los Angeles, was afraid of flying. Facing a deadline, Jack had no choice but to board a train to begin the journey. The two men were seen walking through the middle of this concourse as they headed for the train.

Like all transportation hubs, Grand Central Station is a place of constant comings and goings. Look toward the handsome staircase leading down from the Vanderbilt Avenue entrance that you very recently descended.

15. Grand Central Station. Staircase to West Balcony and Vanderbilt Avenue. If you look hard enough, you may be able to picture Clark Kellogg (Matthew Broderick) tumble down these stairs with all his luggage. Luckily for Clark, or so he thought at the time, he was helped to his feet by con man Victor Ray (Bruno Kirby), in *The Freshman*.

Now, look slightly to your right, to the entrance to track 29.

16. Grand Central Station. Entrance to Track 29. While Clark Kellogg was just arriving, Tom Wingo (Nick Nolte) was escorting his young football protégé Bernard (Jason Gould) to his train, in *The Prince of Tides*. Tom taught Bernard a great deal about football and about life. Thanks to Tom, Bernard might one day be a decent football player, but he was already an accomplished violinist. As they stood before the entrance to this track, Bernard complied with Tom's wishes and showed him and numerous onlookers just how accomplished his musical ability was.

From the magical to the ordinary, the slapstick to the sublime, the happy to the poignant, Grand Central Station has seen it all. The last stop within the terminal is the escalator bank heading north into the MetLife Building.

17. Grand Central Station. Escalator Bank to North Balcony and 45th Street. Charlie Grigante (Al Pacino) was trying to flee from the men who were trying to kill him, as well as from the life of violence he had always lived, in *Carlito's Way*. As his girlfriend Gail (Penelope Ann Miller) waited by the train, Charlie (*aka* Carlito) tried to sneak down these escalators. But he was spotted and a climactic shootout took place on and around this escalator bank.

Time to leave the "Crossroads of a Million Private Lives" that is Grand Central Station. As you face the escalators, turn right and walk toward the Lexington Avenue exit of the terminal. Once outside, get to 43rd Street. You now have a decision to make. You may set off on the brief Tudor City Detour,[3] which will take you a few blocks east, toward the United Nations. If you choose to bypass the detour, skip locations 18 through 21, and follow the directions to location 22. If you choose to take the detour, you are a true adventurer and will be rewarded with some choice movie locations situated in and around Tudor City, one of the most beautiful architectural enclaves in all of New York City.

Before you take another step, look up at the legendary Chrysler Building, which juts majestically into the sky at the corner of Lexington and 42nd Street. Look fast, because that building was another of New York's landmarks that met its maker, in *Armageddon*, when the earth was hit with debris from outer space.

———•—•———

Cross Lexington Avenue and walk east on 43rd Street. It's the only direction you can go on 43rd from Lexington. Cross Second Avenue and continue east until you reach the very end of the street. Walk to the railing overlooking First Avenue below.

18. 43rd Street and First Avenue. The United Nations. The heart of international politics, the United Nations, rising above its picturesque surroundings and the East River, is, with all its familiarity, breathtaking. The Secretariat, the tallest building in the U.N. complex, is where the lovely Emily Taylor (Gwyneth Paltrow) worked as an interpreter, in *A Perfect Murder.*

———•—•———

Look directly down the staircase that leads from where you stand.

19. 43rd Street and First Avenue. From this

---

[3] The Tudor City Detour should take approximately 20 minutes.

vantage point, artist David Shaw (Viggo Mortensen) watched Emily Taylor, with whom he was having an affair, standing with her husband Steven (Michael Douglas), sharing more apparent affection than David had expected to see, in *A Perfect Murder*.

Leave the railing and walk along the buildings on Tudor City Place (do not head back on 43rd Street). Stop when you reach the bridge that spans 42nd Street.

20. Tudor City, above 42nd Street. Atop this overpass is where Rollie Tyler (Bryan Brown) stood with Colonel Mason to discuss whether Rollie would participate in the "fictitious" murder of an organized crime kingpin, DiFranco (Jerry Orbach), in *F/X*.

Walk the short distance to 25 Tudor Place.

21. 25 Tudor Place. Tudor Tower. Allen Bauer (Tom Hanks) had a thriving produce business but lacked a meaningful relationship with anyone except maybe his brother Freddie (John Candy).

Then the woman of Allen's dreams walked into his life. Or, more accurately, swam into his life. The movie? *Splash*, and at least for awhile, Allen lived here together with his soulmate Madison (Daryl Hannah).

Retrace your steps to 43rd Street. Turn left on 43rd and walk west to Lexington Avenue. Turn right on Lexington and head north until you reach 46th Street. Turn left on 46th and walk west, crossing Park Avenue, until just before reaching Madison Avenue.

22. Madison Avenue and 46th Street (Roosevelt Hotel).

Tailing suspects, the detectives Doyle and Russo (Gene Hackman and Roy Scheider, respectively), along with several of their colleagues, followed a man into this hotel, as the Frenchman (Fernando Rey) exited from the other side, in *The French Connection.*

Not realizing that his troubles were just beginning, Michael Jordan (Gene Wilder) shared a cab with the attractive yet evasive Janet Dunn (Kathleen Quinlan), who got out here, in *Hanky Panky.* Later on, as the plot thickened and the web around Michael got tighter, he came back here to look for this lovely woman. While sitting at the bar inside the hotel's lobby, he finally spotted her walking by.

Walk to Madison, turn right and head north on Madison to 47th Street. Turn right on 47th and walk one block east to Park Avenue. Turn left on Park and walk halfway up the block until you are in front of 270 Park Avenue.

23. 270 Park Avenue.

A location I am not 100% certain about, I include it with this slight disclaimer. While Brantley Foster never revealed the secret of his success (see Location 3 of this Walking Tour), it was no secret where J. Pierpont Finch (Robert Morse) was getting his ideas: a book entitled "How to Succeed in Business Without Really Trying." Starting as a window washer, Finch climbed the ladder of success for the World Wide Wicket Company, which was located in this building, in *How to Succeed in Business Without Really Trying*.

Walk north to the corner of 49th Street and turn right. Cross Park Avenue and walk north to the entrance of the Waldorf-Astoria hotel.

24. 301 Park Avenue (between 49th and 50th Streets). The Waldorf-Astoria.

On a wild Thanksgiving weekend in Manhattan, Lieutenant Colonel Frank Slade (Al Pacino), with his naive protégé Charlie (Chris O'Donnell), stayed at this glamorous hotel, in *Scent of a Woman*. The weekend turned out to be a wild ride that changed the lives of the two of them forever.

Prince Akeem (Eddie Murphy) came to America to find a bride. Learning that Akeem and Semmi (Arsenio Hall) were going through money very quickly, King Jaffe Joffer (James Earl Jones) came to America and took up temporary residence here until he could find Akeem and bring him home, in *Coming to America*.[4]

The Waldorf was also where Sonny (Kiefer Sutherland) and Pepper (Woody Harrelson), deciding to find themselves a motel, went for a room and what turned out to be a free meal before figuring out their next step, in *The Cowboy Way*.

Continue past the Waldorf, cross 50th Street and walk north half a block.

---

[4] Anyone who has seen this movie will remember the barbershop scenes in Queens, where the feisty and colorful characters wax eloquent about many topics. Some people may remember that Eddie Murphy and Arsenio Hall played many of the characters in the barber shop. Many people may not remember, however, that the lad getting his haircut in the barbershop when Akeem and Semmi first walked in was a young Cuba Gooding, Jr.

25. Park Avenue (between 50ᵗʰ and 51ˢᵗ Streets). St. Bartholomew's Church. In the movie *Arthur*, immature but fun-loving millionaire playboy Arthur Bach (Dudley Moore) was supposed to marry Susan (Jill Eikenberry) in an orchestrated merger between his family's fortunes and hers. Arthur didn't want to marry Susan, however. He wanted to marry Linda (Liza Minnelli), a girl from the wrong side of the tracks. In

the movie's final scene, Arthur announced he wouldn't marry Susan and descended the steps of this church, where the matriarch of the family, Martha (Geraldine Fitzgerald), sat in her Rolls Royce at the curb.

Fans of the television show "Seinfeld" may or may not remember that Jerry's dad Morty (Barney Martin) played Liza Minnelli's father, in *Arthur*.

Continue north on Park Avenue until you are in front of 375 Park Avenue.

26. 375 Park Avenue (at 52ⁿᵈ Street). Tiger Lady J.C. Wyatt (Diane Keaton) was at the top of her field at the ad agency, Sloane, Curtis & Co., in *Baby Boom*. The agency, where J.C.'s job was threatened by upward-climbing Ken (James Spader), was located in this building. Unfortunately for J.C., or so she thought at first, an unexpected arrival would change everything. Forever.

This building is also where the studios for IBC were located. For those who may not remember, IBC was the Scrooge-like network that wanted to air a live version of Charles Dickens's "A Christmas Carol" on Christmas Eve. No wonder, since the show was being overseen by the grinch-like studio head Frank Cross (Bill Murray), in the movie *Scrooged*.

Continue north on Park for one more block.

27. 399 Park Avenue (between 53rd and 54th Streets). The Larrabees lived in a huge mansion on the North Shore of Long Island on a very large estate. But they spent a good deal of their time here—or at least Linus Larrabee (Harrison Ford) did—in *Sabrina*.

Continue north on Park to 54th Street. Turn left on 54th and walk west until you reach the Monkey Bar of the Hotel Elysée.

28. 60 East 54th Street. The Monkey Bar. Having given up on attractive women, Professor Greg Larkin (Jeff Bridges) placed a personal ad in which he declared that looks were not important. Among the responses was one from Professor Rose Morgan (Barbra Streisand). Although Rose's sister had answered the ad on Rose's behalf, Rose agreed to go out with Greg, and on their first date, they dined here, in *The Mirror Has Two Faces*.

Continue west a very short distance until you are across from the plaza of 535 Madison Avenue.

29. 535 Madison Avenue (at 54th Street). After his friends tried to set him up on a date, Jeffrey (Steven Weber) fled their apartment and their good intentions and raced up Madison Avenue, in *Jeffrey*. They finally caught up with him at the plaza of this building where, to the delight of onlookers, Jeffrey agreed to give the date a try. You may remember that one of the onlookers was Camryn Manheim, who plays Eleanor Frutt on television's "The Practice." Then again, you may not.

———•◆•———

Continue heading west across Madison Avenue until you reach Fifth Avenue. Turn left on Fifth Avenue and head south until you reach 53rd Street. Turn left on 53rd and walk the short distance until you are across from 10 East 53rd.

30. 10 East 53rd Street. HarperCollins Building.

Here attorney Dan Gallagher (Michael Douglas) attended a Saturday meeting while his wife and daughter were out of town. At the meeting, he met Alex Forrest (Glenn Close) with whom he later had dinner. Anyone who has seen the movie will never forget what evolved from this encounter, in *Fatal Attraction*.

The building also housed the office of Larry, who was an editor for Marsha (Anjelica Huston), in *Manhattan Murder Mystery*.

———•◆•———

Return to Fifth Avenue and turn left, continuing south until you reach 49th Street. At 49th, cross Fifth Avenue to the other side and head north half a block until you are standing in front of the Rockefeller Center Promenade.

31. Fifth Avenue (between 49th and 50th Streets). Rockefeller Center.

Kevin McAllister (Macaulay Culkin) was lost in New York and had just done battle with the evil Marv (Daniel Stern) and Harry (Joe Pesci), in *Home Alone 2: Lost in New York*. Standing at the edge of this plaza, gazing at the Christmas tree (which won't be there if it isn't December) and the skating rink below, Kevin prayed for the only thing he wanted that Christmas—to be reunited with his family.

———•◆•———

Note the building in front of you: the tallest structure around.

32. 30 Rockefeller Plaza. In this building were located the offices of the Federal Broadcasting Company. In those offices, efficiency expert Richard Sumner (Spencer Tracy) and Reference Department head Miss Watson (Katharine Hepburn) first battled, then fell in love, in *Desk Set*.

More recently, Benjy Stone (Mark Linn-Baker) recounted his favorite year, when he was a writer for "The Comedy Cavalcade," starring Stan "King" Kaiser (Joseph Bologna), and the week that screen legend Alan Swann (Peter O'Toole) was a guest on the show, in *My Favorite Year*. Benjy worked in this building, where the television show was filmed.

More recently still, "Twenty-One," the focus of the quiz show scandals of the 1950s, was televised from studios within this building, in *Quiz Show*.

Circle the skating rink and, facing 30 Rockefeller Plaza, turn right and walk to the street. Look left, to the awning for NBC Studios.

33. NBC Studios. Rockefeller Center. 50th Street Entrance. Having just gotten his sidekick fired for an antic that backfired, Howard Stern followed a furious Robin Quivers (both playing themselves) outside this NBC entrance onto 50th Street, in *Private Parts*. Robin wanted Howard to quit in protest, but Howard argued that he could

Tour 7

be more effective at winning her back her job by staying at the station.

Turn away from NBC and walk east on 50th Street back to Fifth Avenue. Turn left on Fifth and walk north half a block, until you reach 630 Fifth Avenue (between 50th and 51st Streets). The building is the one with the statue of Atlas out front, holding up the world.

34. 630 Fifth Avenue. The Atlas Building.

Fighting a deadline as usual, this one involving corruption in the garbage industry, Jack Taylor raced to this building to drop off his daughter Maggie (Mae Whitman) and Sam (Alex D. Linz), the son of Melanie Parker (Michelle Pfeiffer), in *One Fine Day*. Fully expecting Jack to be late, Melanie smiled broadly as she descended the escalator inside, seeing Jack and the children right on time.

In another scene from another movie filmed in the lobby and outside this building, Peter Fallow (Bruce Willis) and Albert Fox (Clifton James) rode down the escalators and exited the building, discussing the story of the hit-and-run incident in the Bronx, in *The Bonfire of the Vanities*. By time they reached the statue of Atlas, Fox had pretty much convinced Peter that there was a great book in the incident, and that the book could salvage Peter's career. Fox was right on both counts.

Journalist Phil Green (Gregory Peck) stood before the statue with his son, Tom (Dean Stockwell), in *Gentleman's Agreement*. Phil explained that Atlas was holding the world up on his shoulders. Tom revealed that his grandmother had said the same thing about Phil.

If the building is open, you can go in to see the escalators and the lobby, after which you can move on to the final stop of **Walking Tour 7: Midtown**.

Walk north on Fifth Avenue to the corner of

52nd Street, and turn left on 52nd, heading west until you are across from number 21.

35. 21 West 52nd Street. The 21 Club. This famous restaurant, a New York location that makes frequent screen appearances, the 21 Club has seemingly been around forever. In *Sweet Smell of Success*, ruthless tabloid columnist J.J. Hunsecker (Burt Lancaster) held court at his usual table inside, with the like of senators, aspiring singers and sleazy press agent Sidney Falco (Tony Curtis).

Fresh from the success of his first "tip" to Gordon Gecko (Michael Douglas), Bud Fox (Charlie Sheen) met Gordon for a power lunch here, in *Wall Street*. After recommending the steak tartare, Gordon gave Bud a check for $1,000,000 to invest, in what looked like the beginning of a beautiful friendship.

In another film, later in the day, in the lounge area near the front of the restaurant, another power meeting was taking place. Melanie Parker sat having drinks with her boss and clients, in *One Fine Day*. But Melanie was getting increasingly anxious. The longer she sat there, the less likely she would be able to get her son and Jack Taylor's daughter to Central Park (see **Walking Tour 6: Central Park**) for the big soccer game, where the kids were to get end-of-the-season trophies.

As the 21 Club is a popular place for meetings and celebrations, Laurel Ayres (Whoopi Goldberg) staged a meeting here involving her supposed partner, the fictional Robert S. Cutty, in *The Associate*, and Carol and Larry took their son Nick (Zach Braff) here to celebrate Nick's birthday, in *Manhattan Murder Mystery*.

You have now reached the end of **Walking Tour 7: Midtown**. You are only a few blocks from the starting points for **Walking Tour 1: 57th Street Shopper's Delight**, **Walking Tour 2: The (Lower) Upper West Side** and **Walking Tour 8: Broadway and Beyond**. Take your pick.

Tour 7

Walking Tour 8

BROADWAY AND BEYOND

UPTOWN

WEST
SIDE

EAST
SIDE

DOWNTOWN

TENTH AVE.

NINTH AVE.

EIGHTH AVE.

BROADWAY

SEVENTH AVE.

AVE. AMERICAS

W. 57TH ST.

1

3

2

5

4

6

18

17

16

15

14 13

12 11

9

8 7

10

W. 42ND ST.

21

19

20

Walking Tour 8
BROADWAY AND BEYOND

This beating heart of New York is not only home to one of the greatest concentrations of live theater in the world, but also the home of numerous movie locations.

Walking Tour 8: Broadway and Beyond begins at the intersection of 57th Street and Broadway. If you choose to get to the starting point by public transportation, you may use any of the following subway or bus lines (although the following list is by no means exhaustive):

FROM THE NORTH
SUBWAYS

- **1, 9, A, B, C** or **D** southbound to 59th Street/Columbus Circle. Walk south on Broadway to 57th Street.

BUSES

- **M5** southbound on Riverside Drive, then Broadway, to Columbus Circle. Walk south on Broadway to 57th Street.

- **M7** southbound on Columbus Avenue, then Broadway, to Columbus Circle. Walk south on Broadway to 57th Street.

- **M10** southbound on Central Park West to Columbus Circle. Walk south on Broadway to 57th Street.

- **M104** southbound on Broadway to 57th Street.

FROM THE SOUTH
SUBWAYS

- **1, 9, A, B, C** or **D** northbound to 59th Street/Columbus Circle. Walk south on Broadway to 57th Street.

- **N** or **R** northbound to Seventh Avenue and 57th Street. Walk west on 57th to Broadway.

BUSES

- **M5**, **M6** or **M7** northbound on Avenue of the Americas to 57th Street. Walk west on 57th to Broadway.

- **M10** northbound on Hudson Street, then Eighth Avenue, to 57th Street. Walk east on 57th to Broadway.

- **M11** northbound on Tenth Avenue to 57th Street. Transfer to **M31** or **M57** eastbound to Broadway.

- **M104** westbound on 42nd Street, then northbound on Eighth Avenue, to 57th Street. Walk east on 57th to Broadway.

FROM THE EAST
SUBWAYS

- **N** or **R** westbound to Seventh Avenue and 57th Street. Walk west on 57th to Broadway.

- **7** or **42nd Street Shuttle** westbound to Times Square. Transfer to **1** or **9** northbound to 59th Street/Columbus Circle. Walk south on Broadway to 57th Street.

BUSES

- **M31** or **M57** westbound on 57th Street to Broadway.

FROM THE WEST
BUSES

- **M31** or **M57** eastbound on 57th Street to Broadway.

Starting at the intersection of Broadway and 57th Street, walk south on Broadway until you get to 56th Street. Cross to the east side of Broadway (if you are not there already), and walk south until you are in front of 1740 Broadway.

1. 1740 Broadway. MONY Building. Nervous about introducing his girlfriend Lisa (Mia Farrow) to his overbearing, intrusive mother, Sheldon

(Woody Allen) waited outside this building for Lisa before bringing her to meet his mother, in the "Oedipus Wrecks" segment of *New York Stories*.

Continue south on Broadway to 54th Street. Turn right on 54th and walk west until you reach the legendary Studio 54, just east of Eighth Avenue.

2. 254 West 54th Street. Studio 54. Now serving as a theatre ("Cabaret," at the time this book went to press), this is where it all happened on those boogie nights and last days of disco during the high-flying 1980s of flying high New York. Here Steve Rubell ruled with an iron fist, and bouncers decided whether an aspiring denizen of the night would be welcomed into the inner sanctum of paradise or left to pine away in the street, all brought to life in the movie *54*.

Return to Broadway, turn left and head north to 55th Street. Turn right on 55th and walk east to

Seventh Avenue. Turn right on Seventh and stop in front of Carnegie Deli.

3. 854 Seventh Avenue. Carnegie Deli. In *Broadway Danny Rose*, a number of comedians sat around a table in this restaurant and told stories about hard-luck talent manager Danny Rose (Woody Allen). One of the comedians told the definitive Danny Rose story, which became the film's plot. At the end Danny caught up with Tina (Mia Farrow) in front of Carnegie Deli on a cold, bleak Thanksgiving Day.

In *One Fine Day*, Melanie Parker (Michelle Pfeiffer) and Jack Taylor (George Clooney) were rushing to get Melanie's son Sammy (Alex D. Linz) and Jack's daughter Maggie (Mae Whitman) to a soccer game in Central Park. If the kids didn't play in the game, they didn't get trophies. As they ran up Avenue of the Americas, having just left the 21 Club (see **Walking Tour 7: Midtown**), little Maggie said she had to use the bathroom. As the next exterior shot clearly showed, Jack and young Sammy waited outside this restaurant while Melanie and Maggie were in the bathroom, presumably inside.

———

Head south on Seventh Avenue to 54th Street. Turn left on 54th and walk east until just before Sixth Avenue.

4. 6th Avenue and 54th Street. Hilton Hotel. Much to the dismay of his friends and followers, Malcolm X (Denzel Washington), whose life was believed to be in danger, took a room here to get some work done, in *Malcolm X*.

———

Retrace your steps to Seventh Avenue and turn left. Head south until you are halfway between 53rd and 54th Streets. Look across Seventh Avenue.

5. 834 Seventh Avenue. The Stage Deli. Jeffrey Anderson (Kevin Kline) had been brought back to New York and into the cast of the soap opera "The Sun Also Sets," in order to drive his old flame Celeste (Sally Field) insane, in *Soapdish*. While on the set, Jeffrey asked out the aspiring young starlet Lori Craven (Elisabeth Shue), and then took her to the Stage Deli for dinner.

Head south just to the next corner.

6. 811 Seventh Avenue. Sheraton New York Hotel. High-priced call girl Elizabeth Black (Nancy Allen) had just left a customer at this hotel and, as she exited, found herself being followed by someone who looked eerily like the platinum blonde she had seen standing over the body of Kate Miller (Angie Dickinson) in the elevator, in *Dressed to Kill*. The ensuing chase led to the subway. Fans of Dennis Franz will find him playing a familiar role: that of a cop.

Continue south on Seventh Avenue. At 44th Street, make a left and head east to 111 West 44th.

7. 111 West 44th Street. Belasco Theatre. Having finally found a backer for his show, David Shayne (John Cusack) was able to stage his play "God of Our Fathers" at this theatre. Unfortunately, the funding came with certain strings attached, in Woody Allen's *Bullets Over Broadway*.

Head back west on 44th. Stop at 145 West 44th Street.

8. 145 West 44th Street. Millennium Broadway. In town on business, Max (Wesley Snipes) got more than he bargained for when he stayed at this hotel for an extra night, in *One Night Stand*. As the movie began, he left the hotel and walked west on 44th Street (the same direction you will

soon be heading), as he narrated his tale to the camera.

Continue west on 44th. When you reach Seventh Avenue, cross halfway (there's a median between Seventh and Broadway), pause for only a second, then continue across Broadway. Once you reach the far side of Broadway, you may safely turn and look back at the median you just passed.

9. 44th Street Median (between Broadway and Seventh). Their trip to Yankee Stadium having gone horribly wrong, the patients from Cedarbrook Hospital, Billy (Michael Keaton), Jack (Peter Boyle), Henry (Christopher Lloyd) and Albert (Stephen Furst) found themselves lost in New York without their chaperone. Caught in the rain, they made their way across this intersection, with an empty refrigerator carton over their collective heads, in *The Dream Team*.

Walk slightly south on Broadway and stop in front of 1501.

10. 1501 Broadway. In their effort to take Manhattan by storm, the Muppets approached Broadway producer Martin Price (Dabney Coleman), hoping he would want to produce their show, "Manhattan Melodies." Mr. Price's offices were located in this building, in *The Muppets Take Manhattan*.

Head north to 44th Street. Make a left on 44th and walk west until you are in front of 234 West 44th.

11. 234 West 44th Street. Sardi's. Another scene from *The Muppets Take Manhattan*. In this one, Kermit the Frog sneaked a framed picture of himself, a "famous Broadway producer," onto the wall. Then he sat at a table and waited for his friends to point out to the other restaurant patrons that he, the famous producer, was amongst them.

Continue the short distance west until you are across from the Majestic Theatre.

12. 245 West 44th Street. Majestic Theatre. Things had been going so well for C.C. "Bud" Baxter (Jack Lemmon). By lending out the key to his apartment to his supervisors and bosses at the insurance company where he worked, he was rising fast in the company. However, Bud hit a snag when his big boss, Mr. Sheldrake (Fred MacMurray), wanted to use the apartment for a rendezvous with Fran (Shirley MacLaine), on whom Bud had developed a huge crush. One evening, Bud waited in front of this theatre ("The Music Man" was playing) for Fran to show up. The movie was *The Apartment*.

Head east. Turn left at the Shubert Theatre and walk through Shubert Alley to 45th Street. You'll be standing at the Booth Theatre.

13. 222 West 45th Street. Booth Theatre. During a performance of "Carousel" at this theatre, Mayor John Pappas (Al Pacino) and politico Frank Anselmo (Danny Aiello) met privately to discuss the shooting death of a small child and its larger ramifications, in *City Hall*.

—————•◆•—————

Continue a few steps west, to the Plymouth Theatre.

14. 236 West 45th Street. Plymouth Theatre.

Finally agreeing to play the role of a mother, Elise Eliot (Goldie Hawn) appeared in the play "Of a Certain Age," in *The First Wives Club*. The show, which proved to be a hit, was staged at this theatre.

—————•◆•—————

Head back east to Broadway. Turn left on Broadway and walk north to 46th Street. At the intersection, look toward the Seventh Avenue lanes (the near lanes are Broadway), just north of 46th Street.

15. 46th Street and Seventh Avenue. Intersection.

Injured in a shootout on the subway and ratted on by a cabdriver, Frank White (Christopher Walken) sat bleeding in the backseat of a taxicab at this intersection, in *King of New York*. As the police inched closer to the cab, guns drawn, Frank relinquished his title and slumped in the back seat. He was King of New York no more.

—————•◆•—————

Walk west on 46th Street. Stop across from the first theatre in from the corner.

16. 205 West 46th Street. Lunt–Fontanne Theatre.

Frank White was there to see a show, but the police had other ideas. Confronting Frank in the lobby, several cops (including those played by Wesley Snipes and David Caruso) took Frank outside for a "talking to," in *King of New York*.

—————•◆•—————

Continue west on 46th Street until you get to Eighth Avenue. Look to the northeast corner.

17. Eighth Avenue and 46th Street. McHale's. In many movies about cops, there is a local bar where the officers congregate after a shift. This establishment was frequented by Charlie (Woody

Harrelson), John (Wesley Snipes), Grace (Jennifer Lopez) and a lot of other transit cops, in *Money Train*.

In this same establishment, two young men whose lives had been changed forever—first by a mischievous prank that went wrong and second by the brutality of a reform school guard—exacted their revenge on that guard, Sean Nokes (Kevin Bacon), as he sat eating his meal. John (Ron Eldard) and Tommy (Billy Crudup) recognized him, reminded him of his transgressions, and brutally shot him dead, in *Sleepers*.

Cross Eighth Avenue and head west on 46th Street. Stop across from Barbetta, at 321 West 46th.

18. 321 West 46th Street. Barbetta. Their affair in full swing, bored housewife Alice Tate (Mia Farrow) and her paramour Joe (Joe Mantegna) shared a late lunch here, with no other patrons in sight, in *Alice*. After the meal, Alice shared something else with Joe—a secret potion given to her by her herbalist, Dr. Yang—that turned Alice and Joe invisible.

Continue west on 46th Street until you reach Tenth Avenue. Turn left on Tenth and head south to 42nd Street. Turn left on 42nd and stop across from the National Video Center.

19. 460 West 42nd Street. National Video Center. This is the studio where the soap opera "Southwest General," starring Julie Nichols (Jessica Lange) and unlikely feminist Dorothy Michaels (Dustin Hoffman), was taped, in *Tootsie*. At the end of the movie, Dorothy a thing of the

past, Michael Dorsey (Dustin Hoffman) waited for Julie outside this building. When Julie emerged, Michael followed her east on 42nd Street and they paused to talk, a short distance away.

Continue east to Ninth Avenue. Cross Ninth, make a right and head south on Ninth until you are halfway between 38th and 39th Streets. Look across Ninth.

20. 511 Ninth Avenue. Supreme Macaroni Co. Professional hit man Leon (Jean Reno) was a simple man. He slept on the floor and seemed to care only for his houseplant. Not a man of material needs, he left Tony (Danny Aiello) in charge of his money, which he earned for carrying out "assignments" for Tony, in *The Professional*. On a few occasions, Leon visited Tony at his day job in this restaurant.

Return to 42nd Street, walking up Ninth Avenue, and make a right. Walk east on 42nd until you get to Eighth Avenue. At Eighth, make a quick right.

21. Port Authority Terminal. Eighth Avenue and 42nd Street. Fresh off the farm and eager to make his way in the big city, young Brantley Foster (Michael J. Fox) took his first steps on the

streets of New York when he exited the Port Authority bus terminal and emerged from this entrance, in *The Secret of My Success*.

You have now reached the end of **Walking Tour 8: Broadway and Beyond**. Please consult this book for other Walking Tours. I will not rest until all TourWalkers know this small island of Manhattan as well as I do.

Walking Tour 9
MANHATTAN'S MIDSECTION

While it is not geographically accurate, for convenience sake I've given the name "Manhattan's Midsection" to several contiguous parts of town (Chelsea, Union Square, Gramercy Park, Murray Hill) that have nothing in common except that they are in the lower middle of Manhattan, with no water anywhere in sight. Although there are not as many locations in this Walking Tour as in most of the others, the ones included illustrate the great diversity of films that have been shot in New York.

Walking Tour 9: Manhattan's Midsection begins at the intersection of Eighth Avenue and 14th Street. If you choose to get to the starting point by public transportation, you may use any of the following subway or bus lines (although the following list is by no means exhaustive):

FROM THE NORTH
SUBWAYS
- **A, C** or **E** southbound to 14th Street and Eighth Avenue.
- **1, 2, 3** or **9** southbound to 14th Street. Walk west on 14th to Eighth Avenue.

BUSES
- **M10** southbound on Central Park West, then Broadway, then Seventh Avenue, to 14th Street. Walk west on 14th to Eighth Avenue.
- **M11** southbound on Columbus Avenue, then Ninth Avenue, to 14th Street. Walk east on 14th to Eighth Avenue.

FROM THE SOUTH
SUBWAYS

- **A, C** or **E** northbound to 14th Street and Eighth Avenue.
- **1, 2, 3** or **9** northbound to 14th Street and Seventh Avenue. Walk west on 14th to Eighth Avenue.

BUSES

- **M5** or **M6** northbound on Avenue of the Americas to 14th Street. Walk west on 14th to Eighth Avenue.
- **M10** northbound on Hudson Street, then Eighth Avenue, to 14th Street.

FROM THE EAST
SUBWAYS

- **L** (14th Street Shuttle) westbound to Eighth Avenue.

BUSES

- **M14** westbound on 14th Street, to Eighth Avenue.

FROM THE WEST
BUSES

- **M14** eastbound on 14th Street, to Eighth Avenue.

From Eighth Avenue and 14th Street, walk south on Eighth Avenue (bears slightly to the right) and make a right on Horatio Street. Head west to Washington Street. Turn left on Washington and head south two blocks to 12th Street.

1. 767 Washington Street (at 12th Street). Tortilla Flats. With his brother's marriage a shambles for many reasons, why did Mickey Fitzpatrick (Ed Burns) rush into marrying Hope (Maxine Bahns) a day or two after they met? Good question, but hopeless romantics may know the answer off the tops of their heads. When Hope wasn't eloping with the first cab

driver who came along, she spent her time working in this restaurant, in *She's the One.*

Turn left on 12th Street and walk east until
you reach Eighth Avenue. Turn left on Eighth and
walk north until you reach the northeast corner
of Eighth Avenue at 17th Street.

2. 267 West 17th Street. Chelsea Gym. Having decided to swear off sex and devote all of his
physical energy to working out, Jeffrey (Steven
Weber) worked out at this gym, in *Jeffrey.* Unfor-

tunately for him, Jeffrey found himself drawn to
Steve (Michael T. Weiss), the man who offered to
spot Jeffrey while he lifted weights. And the feeling was mutual. Very mutual.

Continue north on Eighth Avenue until you get to 21st Street. Note the coffee shop on the northeast corner.

3. 216 Eighth Avenue. Bright Food Shop. After getting flowers from an anonymous suitor and then spotting the florist Lewis (Christian Slater) standing beneath her window one night, Lisa (Mary Stuart Masterson) was understandably jumpy. She went to the flower shop to confront Lewis, but they ended up sharing a meal here, in *Bed of Roses*.

Turn left on 21st Street and stop across from 303 West 21st Street.

4. 303 West 21st Street. Things were going well for ambitious Kate (Jennifer Aniston), in *Picture Perfect*, but in the eyes of her boss, they would go a lot better if she were in a stable relationship and more grounded. Rising to the challenge, she arranged to have Nick (Jay Mohr) pose as her fiancé for an important dinner with her boss. Nick, who was from Boston, stayed with Kate in her apartment, which was located in this building. Unfortunately for Nick, however, he slept on the couch.

Walk back to Eighth Avenue. Cross to the east side of Eighth and turn left. Walk north on Eighth to 23rd Street and make a right on 23rd. Stop in front of the Chelsea Hotel, at 222 West 23rd.

5. 222 West 23rd Street. Chelsea Hotel. He may not have been to everyone's taste, but Elizabeth (Kim Basinger) was attracted to John (Mickey Rourke) and his sexual games and fetishes. Until he crossed over the line. In *Nine 1/2 Weeks*, Elizabeth met John here, as per his instructions. But when their latest "session" was to

include another woman, Elizabeth realized it was time to rethink the relationship.

Continue east on 23rd Street until you get to the east side of Avenue of the Americas. Turn right and walk south until you are halfway between 20th and 21st Streets.

6. 664 Avenue of the Americas. Lemon & Lime Coffee Shop. Sheldon (Woody Allen) was at his wit's end. For several weeks, he endured the humiliation of having his mother appear as an apparition over the city, giving advice, revealing things about him to the general populace, and just plain ruining his life, in the "Oedipus Wrecks" segment of *New York Stories*. As Sheldon walked up the street in front of this coffee shop, he was teased by construction workers in hard hats, who, mimicking his mother, inquired as to whether he was dressed warmly enough.

Turn back and head north on Avenue of the Americas until you reach 24th Street.

7. 729 Avenue of the Americas. Billy's. Worm (Edward Norton) was just out of prison and had some outstanding debts to pay, as he learned the hard way, courtesy of a beating from Grama (Michael Rispoli), in *Rounders*. Worm had come into this establishment to kill a little time, and Grama, instead, almost killed him.

Head south on Avenue of the Americas to 23rd Street. Make a left and walk east on 23rd until you are across from 32 West 23rd.

8. 32 West 23rd Street. Beyond the entrance to this building were the corporate offices of MacMillan Toys, the company in which young Josh Baskin (Tom Hanks) climbed the corporate ladder pretty quickly for a thirteen-year-old boy, much to the delight of Mr. MacMillan (Robert Loggia) and Susan (Elizabeth Perkins), and much to the chagrin of Paul (John Heard), in *Big*.

Continue east on 23rd Street to Fifth Avenue. Cross Fifth Avenue but do not cross Broadway. From the small median island, turn and notice the building slightly north of 23rd Street, back across Fifth Avenue.

9. 200 Fifth Avenue. The International Toy Center. Having torn up the private detective's report on the supposed infidelity of his younger wife (Nastassja Kinski) without even reading it, Claude Eastman (Dudley Moore) paid an agitated visit to the private detective (Richard B. Shull) whose office was in this building to request another copy, in *Unfaithfully Yours*.

This building also housed the offices of *The New York Globe*, the paper for which J.J. Hunsecker (Burt Lancaster) wrote his column, in *Sweet Smell of Success*.

From this same vantage point, turn south and note the distinctive and historic Flatiron Building, just south of 23rd Street. Fans of "Veronica's Closet" will recognize the building, which appears frequently in the television show.

10. Intersection Between Flatiron Building and 200 Fifth Avenue. In the intersection, somewhere between the Flatiron Building and 200 Fifth Avenue, biologist Nick (Matthew Broderick) had a plan to lure Godzilla to this spot by dumping truckloads of fish into a huge pile. The plan worked, and the monster in *Godzilla* took the bait. However, he then moved destructively on, so Nick had to come up with another plan.

In an odd twist that I can only presume was intended, in the movie *Armageddon* a vendor stood along this very same intersection, peddling small Godzilla toys, as the first wave of meteorites fell to earth.

———◆◆———

Very carefully (and only where the signs permit), cross 23rd Street and head south on Fifth Avenue. At this intersection, several roads come together, so make sure you head south on Fifth Avenue, rather than Broadway. Continue south on Fifth Avenue until you reach 85 Fifth (between 16th and 17th Streets).

11. 85 Fifth Avenue. This building is where Lenny (Woody Allen) worked as a sportswriter, in *Mighty Aphrodite*.

———◆◆———

Head back north to 17th Street and make a right. Walk east on 17th until you reach Union Square. You should see Union Square Park, slightly to your right. Continue east on 17th Street and stop across from Barnes & Noble.

12. 33 East 17th Street. Barnes & Noble. Was Jerry (Mel Gibson) crazy, or was everyone really out to get him? In *Conspiracy Theory*, we are not quite sure, but after his purchase of "The Catcher in the Rye" at this book store set off an alarm that had him quickly chased by men on motorcycles and in helicopters, we find ourselves thinking that maybe he wasn't crazy after all.

———◆◆———

Continue east along 17th Street. Cross Park Avenue South (also named Union Square East) and continue one more block to Irving Place. Make a left and head north on Irving Place to Gramercy Park South (the same as 20th Street). Private and gated Gramercy Park will be directly in front of you, and since you won't have the keys to get you in, you have no choice but to turn. Turn left and walk the short distance until you are in front of 15 Gramercy Park South. The National Arts Club building should be just to your left.

13. 15 Gramercy Park South (20th Street).

Certain that her neighbor, Mr. House (Jerry Adler), had killed his wife (Lynn Cohen), bored housewife Carol (Diane Keaton) sat in the window facing this street, discussing the "case" with Ted (Alan Alda), in *Manhattan Murder Mystery*. Just after Ted left, Carol was certain she saw the sup-

posedly deceased Mrs. House pass by the window on a public bus. The revelation renewed her interest in the "murder," and even convinced her husband Larry (Woody Allen) to join her in a stakeout.

Continue heading west on Gramercy Park South until you come to Park Avenue South. Turn right on Park Avenue South and walk north until you reach 24th Street. Look diagonally across the intersection.

14. 330 Park Avenue South (at 24th Street).

The massive building on the northwest corner of this intersection, with its high metal gates along both 24th Street and Park Avenue, is one of the more imposing structures in this part of Manhattan. Three years before, Perry (Robin Williams) suffered a horrible tragedy, as his wife was gunned down in a trendy restaurant right before his eyes. Since that time, subsisting below a building's boiler room somewhere, he had found little to live for. The only thing that kept him going was Lydia (Amanda Plummer), who worked behind the gates of this building. Every day like clockwork, Perry staked out the front of the building to watch his beloved Lydia leave for lunch. One day, Jack Lukas (Jeff Bridges), his newfound friend and possible savior, waited with him. The movie? *The Fisher King*.

This building is also where Daryll (William Hurt) worked as a janitor, in *Eyewitness*. There he discovered a corpse one night, and there he

began his quest to win the heart of the beautiful television reporter Tony Sokalow (Sigourney Weaver), who showed up to cover the story of the murder.

———•◦•———

Cross Park Avenue South and head west on 24th Street (you should be walking under the elevated passageway that connects Daryll's building with the one directly across 24th Street). At Madison Avenue, make a right and take a long walk to 33rd Street. From this vantage point, turn left toward Fifth Avenue and take in the splendor of the Empire State Building.

15. 350 Fifth Avenue. The Empire State Building. Once but no longer the tallest building in the world, the Empire State Building still reigns as one of the most impressive structures in Manhattan. At the famed observation deck, way at the top, playboy Nicky Ferranti (Cary Grant) waited in vain for shipboard paramour Terry McKay (Deborah Kerr) to show up, in *An Affair to Remember*.

Years later, on that same deck, Annie Reed (Meg Ryan) finally had her rendezvous with widower Sam Baldwin (Tom Hanks), as Sam's euphoric son Jonah (Ross Malinger), who orchestrated their meeting, looked on, in *Sleepless in Seattle*.

And an ape named King Kong, carrying Fay Wray, climbed to the top, in *King Kong*.

Continue up Madison to 35th Street. At 35th, cross Madison to the west side of the street and continue north up Madison until you are halfway between 35th and 36th Streets. Look directly across Madison.

16. 211 Madison Avenue between 35th and 36th Streets. Morgan Court. This towering structure, which seems to cut the sky like a sliver, was home to Carly (Sharon Stone), Jack (Tom Berenger) and, most notably, the privacy-challenged owner of

the building, Zeke (Billy Baldwin), in the 1993 thriller, *Sliver*.

———◆—◆————

Continue north on Madison until you reach the corner of 36th Street. Turn right on 36th Street, cross Madison and walk halfway down the block until you are across from the massive edifice on the north side of the street.

17. 29 East 36th Street. Morgan Library. Coalhouse Walker (Howard E. Rollins, Jr.) had been wronged by the New Rochelle fire department, and especially by Fire Chief Willie Conklin (Kenneth McMillan). Determined to get retribu-

tion—he demanded only that his car be returned, cleaned—Coalhouse and some friends muscled their way in here and waged a standoff, placing the priceless collectibles of J.P. Morgan at risk, in *Ragtime*.

———◆—◆————

You have reached the end of **Walking Tour 9: Manhattan's Midsection**. If you have not already done so, you may take **Walking Tour 7: Midtown**, the starting point of which is only a few blocks from here.

UPTOWN

WEST SIDE   EAST SIDE

DOWNTOWN

7TH AVE.

GREENWICH AVE.

W. 14TH ST.

AVE. AMERICAS

FIFTH AVE.

BROADWAY

FOURTH AVE.

W. 4TH ST.

HUDSON ST.

CHRISTOPHER ST.

GREENWICH ST.

BLEECKER ST.

W. 8TH ST.

LAGUARDIA PL.

LAFAYETTE ST.

HOUSTON ST.

Walking Tour 10
THE VILLAGE

Long considered the home of New York's funkiest and most bohemian life styles, Greenwich Village is rich with winding streets, beautiful brownstones and endless outdoor cafes that can satisfy the most diverse cross-section of tastes from anywhere in the world.

Walking Tour 10: The Village begins at the northeast corner of Broadway and 12th Street. If you choose to get to the starting point by public transportation, you may use any of the following subway or bus lines (although the following list is by no means exhaustive):

FROM THE NORTH
SUBWAYS
- **4, 5, 6, N** or **R** southbound to 14th Street/Union Square.

BUSES
- **M1** southbound on Fifth Avenue, then Park Avenue, then Park Avenue South, to 14th Street.
- **M2, M3** or **M5** southbound on Fifth Avenue to 14th Street. Walk east on 14th to Broadway.
- **M6** or **M7** southbound on Seventh Avenue, then Broadway, to 14th Street.
- **M15** southbound on Second Avenue to 14th Street. Walk west on 14th to Broadway.
- **M101, M102** or **M103** southbound on Lexington Avenue, then Third Avenue, to 14th Street. Walk west on 14th to Broadway.

FROM THE SOUTH
Subways
- **4, 5, 6, N** or **R** northbound to 14th Street/Union Square.

Buses
- **M103** northbound on Bowery, then Third Avenue, to 14th Street. Walk west on 14th to Broadway.

FROM THE EAST
Subways
- **L** (14th Street Shuttle) westbound to Union Square.

Buses
- **M8** westbound on 10th Street, then 9th Street, to Broadway. Walk north on Broadway to 12th Street.
- **M9** or **M14** westbound on 14th Street, to Union Square.

FROM THE WEST
Subways
- **L** (14th Street Shuttle) eastbound to Union Square.

Buses
- **M8** eastbound on 10th Street, then 8th Street, to Broadway. Walk north on Broadway to 12th Street.
- **M14** eastbound on 14th Street to Union Square.

If the point at which you exit either a subway or bus is on 14th Street, find Broadway and head south on Broadway until you reach 12th Street. If you get off a bus at a place other than 14th Street, walk the short distance to 12th Street and Broadway.

1. 828 Broadway (at 12th Street). Ouise (Stockard Channing), Flanders (Donald Sutherland) and friends headed to this branch of the

Strand Book Store, which boasts eight miles of books, looking for an autobiography of Sidney Poitier to find out if their mysterious visitor Paul (Will Smith) was really the famed actor's son, in *Six Degrees of Separation*.

Continue south on Broadway until you reach 10th Street. Turn right on 10th and head west until you are across from 28 East 10th Street.

2. 28 East 10th Street. Devonshire House. One night, newspaper editor Henry (Michael Keaton) returned home to this building, where he lived, to find that his very pregnant wife Martha (Marisa Tomei) had had a complication, in *The Paper*.

Continue west on 10th Street until you get to Fifth Avenue. Turn right on Fifth and walk north until just before 12th Street.

3. 51 Fifth Avenue (at 12th Street). Fans of the hit television series "Mad About You" might recognize this building, with its distinctive colonnade outside the corner window on the second floor, as the home of Paul (Paul Reiser) and Jamie (Helen Hunt) Buchman.

Cross Fifth Avenue and walk west on 12th

Street until you are standing across from 31-33 West 12th Street.

4. 31-33 West 12th Street. Perhaps the secret to winning both an Emmy and an Oscar in the same year is to keep the location-shooting for your movie and television show very close together. While husband Paul was working on one of his many documentaries, Jamie Buchman (Helen Hunt) might have been sneaking out of their apartment, in the building we just left, to visit obsessive-compulsive Melvin Udall (Jack Nicholson), in *As Good As It Gets*, in the building before you now. In one memorable scene, Carol Connelly (Hunt) showed up at Melvin's apartment in a very wet, tight-fitting T-shirt. Of course, maybe Hunt won both her awards because she happens to be a terrific actress. But the proximity of both locations to one another is interesting in any event.

Head back east on 12th Street until you again reach Fifth Avenue. Turn right and head south on Fifth until you reach the restaurant on the right, just before the corner of 9ᵗʰ Street.

5. 24 Fifth Avenue. In *As Good As It Gets*, Melvin Udall, avoiding the cracks on the sidewalk, walked the same route every day to this restaurant. If he was lucky, he sat at the same table.

He unwrapped his sanitary plastic silverware from the protective bag and waited for his favorite waitress Carol to serve him his meal.

———•◦•———

Continue south on Fifth Avenue. Slow down as you approach Washington Square Park (a block south of 8th Street).

6. Washington Square Park. Fifth Avenue Entrance. After driving together to New York City, Harry Burns (Billy Crystal) and Sally Albright (Meg Ryan) parted ways under the shadow of this arch. Harry had said that men and women can't be friends, because sex always gets in the way. Sally told him how unfortunate that was, since Harry was the only person she knew in New York, where she was about to begin law school. They went their separate ways, and it would be five years before their paths crossed again, in *When Harry Met Sally . . . .*

———•◦•———

Enter the park, and walk along the right side of the performance pit in the center of the park.

7. Washington Square Park. Performance Pit. It would be five years before Sally Albright was to see Harry Burns again, and eight years until Meg Ryan, playing Maggie, a jilted lover in *Addicted to Love*, would sit here and plot revenge with fellow jilted lover Sam (Matthew Broderick). A favorite of street performers, the circular performance pit is crowded most weekends with magicians, jugglers and the like. Among the dirty tricks that Sam and Maggie plotted were to put lipstick on a performing monkey and have him kiss the collar of Anton (Tcheky Karyo), for whom Sam's girlfriend Linda (Kelly Preston) had jilted him. Another plot involved having some kids squirt Anton with perfume from their super-soaker water guns.

Interestingly enough, Meg Ryan wasn't the

only one of the two to appear twice in a Washington Square Park movie scene. Years earlier, in *The Freshman*, Matthew Broderick as Clark Kellogg, spotting Victor Ray (Bruno Kirby), the man who had stolen his luggage a few days before, climbed out of a window and chased Victor through this park.

And, if you look hard enough, you may even see Steven Taylor (Michael Douglas) near the performance pit making a payoff of $400,000 to David Shaw (Viggo Mortensen), in return for David's silence about the attempted murder of Steven's wife Emily (Gwyneth Paltrow), in *A Perfect Murder*.

Similarly, if you look really hard, you may see Marina (Demi Moore) try and teach the affable yet uncoordinated Doc (Jeff Bridges) how to rollerskate inside the performance pit, in *The Butcher's Wife*.

Walk toward the right and head toward the southwest corner (the intersection of MacDougal and West 4th Streets). Bear left at the statue of Alexander Lyman Holley. Three asphalt mounds should be on your left. With any luck, you should pass through Chess Table Alley (not the official name).

8. Washington Square Park. MacDougal and West 4th Streets. Chess Table Alley. By watch-

ing Vinnie (Laurence Fishburn) and others play chess at these tables, young Josh Waitzkin (Max Pomeranc) developed both an understanding of and a genuine flair for the game, in *Searching for Bobby Fischer*. Wary at first, Josh's parents (Joan Allen and Joe Mantegna) eventually warmed up to the players and the area, once they realized that all looked upon Josh as perhaps the next Bobby Fischer.

Exit the park past the chess tables, turn left and head south on MacDougal Street.

Continue until you get to the corner of Minetta Lane.

9. 113 MacDougal Street. Minetta Tavern.

He got his childhood friends acquitted of murder charges (no simple task, considering the fact that he was the prosecuting attorney) and afterwards, Michael (Brad Pitt) came here for a secret reunion with the defendants John (Ron Eldard) and Tommy (Billy Crudup), reporter Shakes (Jason Patric) and all-around friend, Carol (Minnie Driver), in *Sleepers*.

Continue south on MacDougal until you get to the corner of MacDougal and Bleecker Streets. Cross Bleecker.

10. Bleecker and MacDougal Streets. Southeast Corner. Le Figaro Cafe.

His conviction finally overturned after he had spent five years in prison, Carlito Grigante (Al Pacino) was anxious to pick up where his life had left off. That included getting re-involved with his one-time girlfriend Gail (Penelope Ann Miller), in *Carlito's Way*. They sat here, at a table near the window along MacDougal Street, and caught up.

Head east on Bleecker Street (away from Sixth Avenue) until you come to LaGuardia Place.

11. Bleecker and LaGuardia Place. Southwest Corner. After taking his niece to a movie, Clifford (Woody Allen) decided to check with his service in *Crimes and Misdemeanors*. He used a pay phone on this corner which (as seems to be the case with most pay phones used in movies) doesn't really exist. Clifford remarked that he's not sure why he bothers calling his service, because he hasn't had a message in seven years, but this time he did. He learned that Professor Levy, the subject of his documentary, had committed suicide.

Continue east on Bleecker until you reach Broadway. Turn left on Broadway and head north until you reach the far side of Bond Street. Turn right on Bond until you are in front of 2 Bond Street. Note the large building directly across the street.

12. 1-5 Bond Street. It took some ingenuity to get their husbands to finance the event, but spurned first wives Elise (Goldie Hawn), Brenda (Bette Midler) and Annie (Diane Keaton) finally held their big benefit for the Cynthia Griffin Center on the first floor of this building, in *The First Wives Club*. Emboldened by Ivana Trump, who had told the ladies "don't get mad, get everything," the three of them knew that life would only get better from that point forward.

Return to Broadway, turn left and walk south until you reach Houston Street. Turn right on Houston, and walk west until you get to 114 West Houston.

13. 114 West Houston Street. Pageant Book and Print Shop. Elliot (Michael Caine) had lusted after his wife's sister Lee (Barbara Hershey) for a long time. One afternoon, he staged a "chance" encounter with her not far from the

building in which she lived. The two of them came to the Pageant, in *Hannah and Her Sisters*. However, in the movie, the book shop may have been situated somewhere other than this location on Houston Street.

———————

Continue walking west on Houston Street until you reach Avenue of the Americas. Turn right on Avenue of the Americas (same as Sixth Avenue) and walk north until you get to Minetta Street. At Minetta, cross Sixth Avenue and walk the short block west to Carmine Street.

14. Bleecker and Carmine Streets. Northwest Corner. While he walked near this corner, bemoaning his rock-bottom social life, but admitting he was not yet ready for a relationship, Sam (Matthew Broderick) fantasized about his dream woman: a Norwegian who spoke no English, was in town for only two weeks and was then flying to Burma to do relief work for the next five years. And, as happens so often in the movies, and especially in *The Night We Never Met*, she appeared, in the guise of the lovely Inga (Dana Wheeler-Nicholson).

———————

Walk north on Carmine Street until you re-merge with Sixth Avenue. Turn left on Sixth and continue walking north until you reach 3rd Street. You should be in front of the Waverly Theatre.

15. 323 Avenue of the Americas. Waverly Theatre. Their mysterious visitor Paul had finally agreed to turn himself in to the police in *Six Degrees of Separation*, but only if Ouise promised to meet him at the Waverly and accompany him. But Ouise and her husband Flanders, delayed by traffic, got to the movie house too late: the police had already apprehended Paul.

This theater was also visible in the background of *Carlito's Way*. While Gail waited in the car across the street, Carlito went to a travel agency to buy the train tickets that would get them out of New York to finally start a new life.

———

Continue north on Sixth Avenue until you are across from the basketball courts on the east side of Sixth Avenue. Just past the basketball courts, stop and walk to the curb.

16. Avenue of the Americas. Just north of basketball courts. At another pay phone that doesn't exist in real life, hard-luck boxing promoter Harry Fabian (Robert DeNiro) made a call to a Mr. Feldman around this spot, with the Washington Square Coffee Shop visible in the distance, in *Night and the City*. The purpose of his call was to get boxing gloves for use in the matches he was promoting.

———

Continue north to Waverly Place. Make a left on Waverly and stop at 149.

17. 149 Waverly Place. Gus's Place. Late as usual and working on a story with a fast-approaching deadline, Henry met his wife Martha and the in-laws here for dinner. Distracted by the deadline and the cacophony caused by kids at a nearby table, Henry decided to skip dinner, leaving his wife none too happy with him, in *The Paper*.

———

Retrace your steps on Waverly and make a left onto Gay Street. Walk the short distance up Gay Street until you reach the white building on the right, just before the large "10" on the window.

18. 17 Gay Street. Charlie Grigante, wanting to resume his relationship with Gail, in *Carlito's Way,*

followed her and found that she lived in this building, down the steps leading from the curb.

———————

Continue to the end of Gay Street and make a left to Christopher Street. Follow Christopher (it bears to the right) until you reach the Stonewall (the bar where the Gay Rights Movement is said to have been born) on the right. Facing Stonewall, look at the building to the left and the steps leading down to a bar.

19. 55 Christopher Street. Although in the movie the bar had a large "M" outside, it was in front of this place that Jeffrey (Steven Weber) ran into his friends Sterling (Patrick Stewart) and Darius (Bryan Batt), who had joined the Pink Panthers to prevent gay-bashing, in *Jeffrey.*

———————

Continue past this bar the short distance to Seventh Avenue South. Turn left and note the entrance to the subway station at Sheridan Square.

20. Sheridan Square. Seventh Avenue and West 4th Street. Subway Entrance. Things had not been going well for Jamie Conway (Michael J. Fox), in *Bright Lights, Big City*. His wife Amanda (Phoebe Cates) had dumped him and he had lost his job as a fact-checker at a prestigious magazine. Now, to top it off, he showed up at the building where he lived to find his brother Michael (Charlie Schlatter) waiting for him. Panicking, Jamie headed for the relative safety of the subway and ran down these stairs.

Look diagonally across Seventh Avenue South.

21. 110 Seventh Avenue South. He may not have been the most successful attorney in the world, but somehow he still believed in doing the honorable thing. And thanks to someone who believed in him unfailingly, Roger Baron (Robert Downey, Jr.), he was still fighting for what was right. His name was Edward J. Dodd (James Woods), and his offices were upstairs behind the door, to the left of Village Cigars, in *True Believer*.

Next, determine which street of all the ones converging at this intersection is West 4th Street, and head east (away from Seventh Avenue South) on West 4th until you reach Barrow Street.

22. 186 West 4th Street. Boxers Restaurant. This restaurant was where Harry Fabian spent much of his free time, in *Night and the City*. It was owned by Helen (Jessica Lange), the married woman with whom Harry was having an affair, and her husband, who happened to be a friend of Harry's. At least the man *thought* Harry was his friend. Just another night in The City.

Turn right on Barrow, cross Seventh Avenue South and make a right on Bleecker Street. At the intersection of Bleecker and Grove, note the restaurant Grove, on the corner. Make a left on Grove and stop outside the side entrance of the restaurant, along the red brick wall.

23. 314 Bleecker Street (at Grove). Harry (Woody Allen) walked along the red brick wall and into this restaurant. He sat down at a table with ex-girlfriend Fay (Elisabeth Shue) and suggested that they try again, but Fay had other ideas. She told him that she was getting married to Harry's one-time friend Larry (Billy Crystal), in *Deconstructing Harry*.

Return to Bleecker and make a right. Turn right on Seventh Avenue South and make a right onto Commerce Street. Walk along Commerce until you get to 50 Commerce.

24. 50 Commerce Street. The Grange Hall. As they emerged from this popular West Village restaurant, so-called writer Barry (Edward Burns) admitted to his lunch companion Marty (Peter Johansen) that he hadn't been able to write. The problem may have stemmed from the difficulties Barry, like his brothers, had with women, in *The Brothers McMullen*.

Continue to the end of Commerce (which merges with Barrow). Make a left on Barrow and walk until you reach Hudson Street. Turn right on Hudson and walk north one block, to Grove Street. Turn right on Grove and walk the short distance until the street curves. Note the building on the next corner.

25. 90 Bedford Street (at Grove). Chez Michallet. This exterior should be familiar to anyone who has become a fan of "Friends," the hit television show. The apartments of Rachel (Jennifer Aniston), Monica (Courtney Cox),

Chandler (Matthew Perry) and Joey (Matt LeBlanc) are located within this building.

Return to Hudson and make a left. Head south on Hudson two blocks, until you come to Morton Street. Turn left on Morton and walk the short distance until you are across from 66 Morton.

26. 66 Morton Street. It seemed like a great arrangement at the time, although one that only New Yorkers may fully understand. About to get married but unwilling to give up his rent-controlled apartment, real estate man Brian

(Kevin Anderson) decided to rent out his apartment to two other people for two nights each. As with all well-laid plans, this one went awry and led to much confusion. The movie is *The Night We Never Met*, and the apartment was located upstairs in this building.

A nosy neighbor often watched the goings-on from the window closest to the front door.

You have now come to the end of **Walking Tour 10: The Village**. The starting point for **Walking Tour 12: SoHo and TriBeCa** is not far from here, so as my guest you may want to continue with the festivities.

Tour 10

Walking Tour 11
THE LOWER ENVIRONS

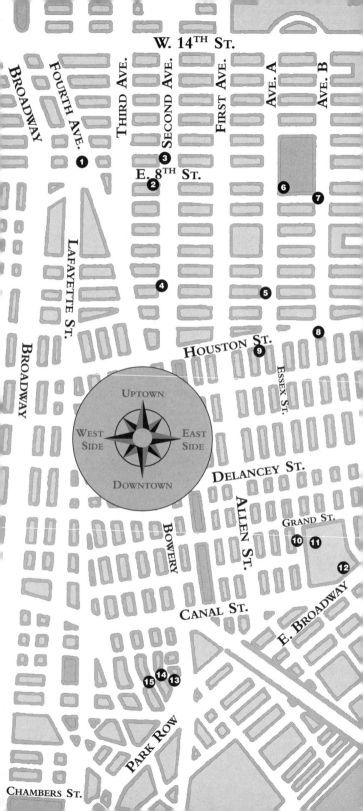

Walking Tour 11
THE LOWER ENVIRONS

This broad cross-section covers several divergent neighborhoods of New York. Each of them—the East Village, the Lower East Side, the Bowery and Chinatown—has its own completely separate flavor and character and their combination makes this the richest and most culturally diverse of the Walking Tours.

Walking Tour 11: The Lower Environs begins at the northeast corner of Fourth Avenue and 9th Street, facing a "square" known as Astor Place. If you choose to get to the starting point by public transportation, you may use any of the following subway or bus lines (although the following list is by no means exhaustive):

FROM THE NORTH
SUBWAYS

- **4, 5** or **6** southbound to 14th Street/Union Square. Switch to **6** southbound to Astor Place.
- **N** or **R** southbound to 8th Street. Walk east on 8th to Astor Place.

BUSES

- **M1** southbound on Fifth Avenue, then Park Avenue, then Park Avenue South, then Broadway, to 9th Street. Walk east on 9th to Fourth Avenue.
- **M2** or **M3** southbound on Fifth Avenue, then eastbound on 8th Street, to Astor Place.
- **M15** southbound on Second Avenue to 9th Street. Walk west on 9th to Fourth Avenue.

- **M101, M102** or **M103** southbound on Lexington Avenue, then Third Avenue, to 9th Street. Walk west on 9th to Fourth Avenue.

FROM THE SOUTH
SUBWAYS
- **6** northbound to Astor Place.
- **N** or **R** northbound to 8th Street. Walk east on 8th to Astor Place.

BUSES
- **M103** northbound on Bowery, then Third Avenue, to 9th Street. Walk west on 9th to Fourth Avenue.

FROM THE EAST
SUBWAYS
- **L** (14th Street Shuttle) westbound to Union Square. Walk south on Fourth Avenue to 9th Street.

BUSES
- **M8** westbound on 10th Street, then 9th Street, to Fourth Avenue.
- **M9** or **M14** westbound on 14th Street, to Union Square. Walk south on Fourth Avenue to 9th Street.

FROM THE WEST
SUBWAYS
- **L** (14th Street Shuttle) eastbound to Union Square. Walk south on Fourth Avenue to 9th Street.

BUSES
- **M8** eastbound on 10th Street, then 8th Street, to Astor Place.
- **M14** eastbound on 14th Street to Union Square. Walk south on Fourth Avenue to 9th Street.

When you get to Astor Place, find the corner of Fourth Avenue and 9th Street. You should be just north of the ornate subway station entrance on the median.

1. Astor Place Subway Entrance. Although the movie ostensibly took place in Hell's Kitchen (see **Walking Tour 8: Broadway and Beyond**), the pivotal scene in *Sleepers* took place right here, quite a distance away. The four young boys, John, Tommy, Michael and Shakes, had a scheme where one of them would order a hot dog from a vendor and then run off without paying, the vendor

would give chase, leaving his hot dog cart unattended and allowing the others to help themselves to the waiting hot dogs. However, the others couldn't resist running off with the cart itself, only to leave it dangling at the top of this subway entrance. When they lost their grip, the cart plummeted down the steps, injuring a man and changing all of their lives forever.

———————

Continue south the short distance to 8th Street (Astor Place), turn left and walk east. Cross Third Avenue and head east on the south side of St. Mark's Place. Stop just before the awning to Dojo Restaurant (24 St. Mark's Place).

2. 24 St. Mark's Place. Dojo Restaurant. Out to add a little adventure to her otherwise humdrum suburban existence, Roberta (Rosanna Arquette) followed the elusive Susan (Madonna) from Battery Park (see **Walking Tour 13: Downtown and Financial District**) to this street, where Roberta accidentally knocked over a vendor's wares, just west of this restaurant, in *Desperately Seeking Susan*.

For those TourWalkers who crave a little sustenance before continuing on this Walking Tour, Dojo is known for its good food and very reasonable prices.

Continue east until you get to Second Avenue. Make a left on Second and stop at 135.

3. 135 Second Avenue. New York Public Library: The Ottendorfer Branch.

This is where Lewis (Christian Slater) came to read to children and to watch as the children were read to, in *Bed of Roses*.

Tour 11

Turn back and head south on Second Avenue until you reach 43 Second Avenue.

4. 43 Second Avenue (between 2nd and 3rd Streets). Provenzano Funeral Home.

Good cop Danny Ciello (Treat Williams) came here to attend the funeral of a murdered relative, in *Prince of the City*, but he was turned away at the door. It seemed that his fellow officers believed that, in agreeing to cooperate with the commission that

was investigating police corruption, he had turned against them.

Return to 3rd Street and cross Second Avenue. Continue east on 3rd Street for two blocks until you reach Avenue A. Turn right on Avenue A and stop in front of Two Boots Pizza.

5. 37 Avenue A. Two Boots Pizza. The movie was *Hi-Life* and bartender Ray (Campbell Scott) was walking around the neighborhood collecting money other bartenders had borrowed from him. He ended up here, engaged in a heated discussion with a grumpy "Santa Claus," and the two of them spilled out onto the street, fighting. However, no matter how much I like the pizza here (it is terrific), I must nominate this location for a NitPick. Why? Because the neighborhood Ray worked in was the Upper West Side (see **Walking Tour 3: The (Upper) Upper West Side**), and how he ended up down here remains a mystery. In fact, when the police broke up the fight, they reported the fight as occurring on Amsterdam Avenue at 84th Street. Unfortunately, poetic license provides no protection against the label of NitPick.

Head north on Avenue A until you reach 7th Street. Tompkins Square Park should be diagonally across 7th Street. Turn right on 7th (keeping the park on your left). Note the southwest corner of the park.

6. Tompkins Square Park (Avenue A and 7th Street). In the movie, there was a fountain (not there in real life, as you can see), but in this corner of the park, John McClain (Bruce Willis) and Zeus (Samuel L. Jackson) struggled to solve a riddle involving jugs and water in order to prevent the detonation of a bomb, in *Die Hard With a Vengeance*.

Continue east on 7th Street until you reach the near corner of Avenue B.

7. Avenue B and 7th Street. Corner Bar. Mick Dundee (Paul Hogan) was out for a night on the town, and he and a cabdriver who had just gotten off duty came here to hoist a few, in *"Croc-odile" Dundee*. Outside the bar, Mick defended the honor of two ladies. Unbeknownst to Mick, however, the ladies were hookers and the man he belted was their pimp.

Turn right on Avenue B and walk south to Houston Street. Cross Houston, turn right and walk west one block to Suffolk Street.

8. East Houston and Suffolk Streets. Meow Mix. Comic book creator Holden McNeil (Ben Affleck) thought he had finally met the woman for him. She invited him to the city one evening to hear her sing. He was soon smitten, but he didn't yet have all the facts. That all changed at this bar, where Holden learned during the course of the evening that Alyssa Jones (Joey Lauren Adams), the object of his crush, was already in-volved—with another woman. The movie is *Chasing Amy*.

Cross Suffolk and continue west three blocks, until you reach Ludlow Street.

9. 205 East Houston (at Ludlow Street). Katz's Delicatessen. Home of some very tasty food, not to mention one of the more memorable scenes in recent movie history. Harry (Billy Crystal) just wanted some corned beef, but Sally (Meg Ryan) gave him, and the rest of the restaurant patrons, a whole lot more—a simulated orgasm, prompting a nearby diner (director Rob Reiner's

real-life mom) to tell a passing waiter, "I'll have what she's having." The movie is *When Harry Met Sally...*, but I suspect I didn't have to tell you that.

A few people who may have missed Sally's performance were sitting around the corner, to the right, in the back of the restaurant. There, undercover F.B.I. agent Joey Pistone, *aka* Donnie Brasco (Johnny Depp), met with fellow agents to discuss the progress and status of his infiltration of local mobs, in *Donnie Brasco*.

If you go inside Katz's, I have no doubt you will enjoy the food. And you might want to mention that my last name is the same as that of the restaurant. Although we are not related and Katz's doesn't sell books, who knows? Anyway, it can't hurt.

Head back the other way, east on Houston for one block, and turn right on Essex Street. At this point, there are several blocks to walk, but they are relatively close together. Continue south on Essex (the east side of the street) until you pass Grand Street. After Grand, slow down and look across Essex until you see 35 Essex.

10. 35 Essex Street. Guss's Pickles. While you crossed Grand to get here, that may not mean much to you. However, you also crossed Delancey. Still not sure? This pickle place is where Sam (Peter Riegert) worked. Occasionally, he hu-

mored Hannah the Matchmaker (Sylvia Miles) who was known to come by with pictures of eligible young women. One such woman, Isabel (Amy Irving), really caught Sam's fancy, in *Crossing Delancey*.

Before you continue heading south on Essex, take a look at the handball courts behind you.

11. Essex Street. Handball Courts. Also featured in *Crossing Delancey*, these courts hosted a game between Sam and a friend, but the game was interrupted by Isabel, who came by to thank Sam for the new hat he had purchased for her.

Continue your southward journey on Essex. Turn left on Canal Street (at Straus Square) and head east until you get to the place where Canal merges with East Broadway. Continue east a slight distance until you get to the entrance of the building on the left, just past Jefferson Street.

12. 192 East Broadway. New York Public Library: Seward Park Branch. She loved to party, which might be where the movie got its name, but Mary (Parker Posey) had a serious side, too. She wanted more than anything to excel in the library sciences. Thanks to a family friend who gave her a job, Mary spent her days working in the library, at this branch, in *Party Girl*.

Head west on East Broadway (back the other way). Do not bear right at Straus Square. Cross Pike Street and continue west through the very colorful Chinatown. Make a right on Catherine Street (just before the statue of Lin Ze Xu). At the intersection of Catherine and Division Streets (Chatham Square), cross over onto Doyers Street. Walk along the curving street until you reach number 18 (on the right hand side).

13. 18 Doyers Street. Alice Tate (Mia Farrow) had it all—a beautiful New York City home, complete with domestic staff, a good-looking, successful husband and adoring children. Or so it seemed to the outside world. For she still was not happy. Far from it. In *Alice*, Alice came here on a regular basis to visit her herbalist, Dr. Yang (Keye Luke), who gave her potions that did some pretty amazing things (see **Walking Tour 4: The Upper East Side**).

Now turn around and admire the singularity of this particular street. Littered with perhaps more barbershops and hair salons per square foot than anywhere else in Manhattan, this street looks as if it were a perpetual movie set.

14. Doyers Street and Pell Street. Intersection. Just about where you are standing, a bloody shootout took place between feuding drug gangs,

led by Frank White (Christopher Walken) on the one side and Larry Wong (Joey Chin) on the other, in *King of New York*.

Continue on to the end of Doyers, where it intersects with Pell Street. Turn left on Pell and walk to the restaurant, just to the left of 22 Pell.

15. Restaurant to Left of 22 Pell Street. Edward J. Dodd (James Woods) was defending a man who had been charged with murder, in *True Believer*. The murder took place right in front of this restaurant.

You have now reached the end of **Walking Tour 11: The Lower Environs**. From here, I might suggest starting on **Walking Tour 10: The Village**, **Walking Tour 12: SoHo and Tri-BeCa** or **Walking Tour 13: Downtown and Financial District**, all of which are relatively close by.

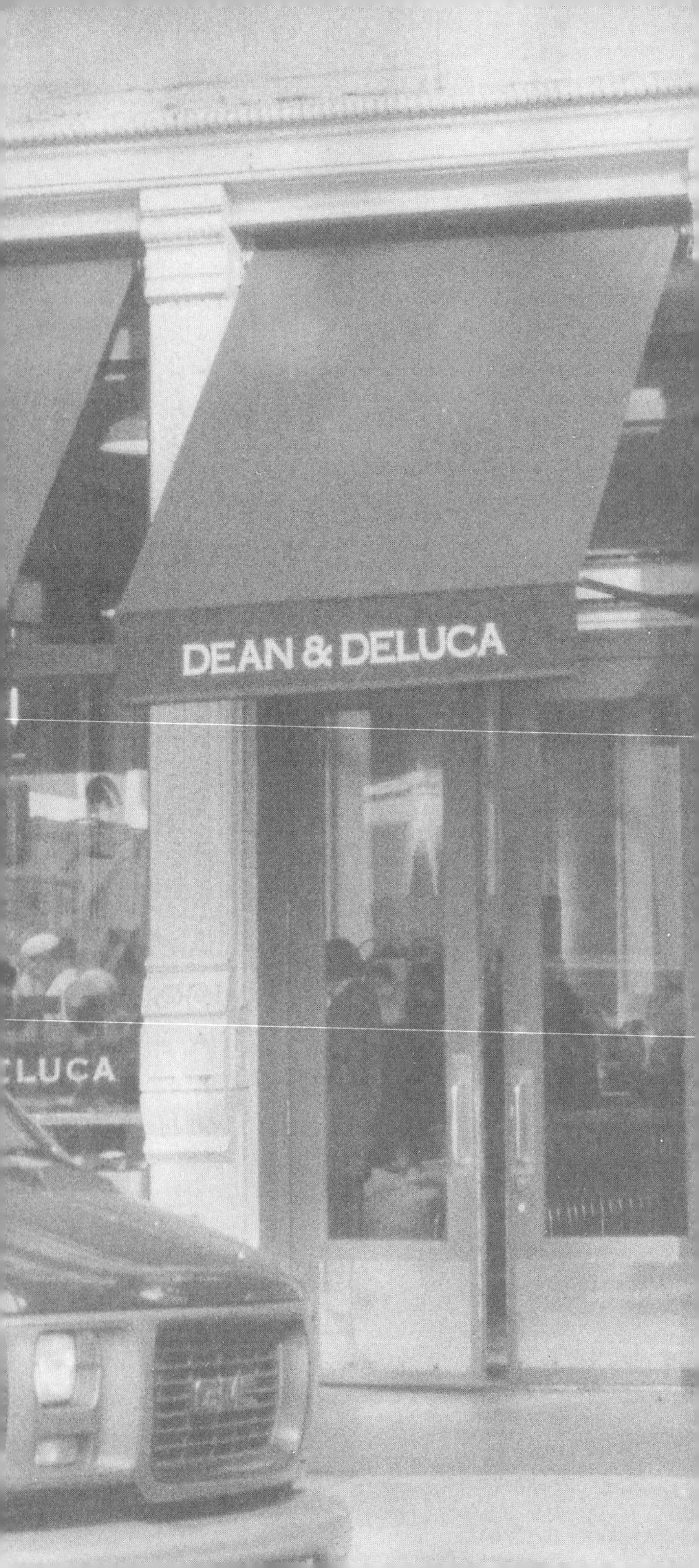
DEAN & DELUCA
LUCA

Walking Tour 12
SOHO AND TRIBECA

Walking Tour 12

SOHO AND TRIBECA

Two of the many acronyms that have sprung up to define, both geographically and culturally, the various areas of Manhattan, are SoHo (South of Houston [Street]) and TriBeCa (Triangle Below Canal [Street]). Both are centers of art and fashion, the chic and the "hip," but they once buzzed in a different way, with manufacturing and industry.

Walking Tour 12: SoHo and TriBeCa begins on West Houston Street and Avenue of the Americas (6th Avenue). If you choose to get to the starting point by public transportation, you may use any of the following subway or bus lines (although the following list is by no means exhaustive):

FROM THE NORTH
SUBWAYS

- **1** or **9** southbound to Houston Street. Walk east on Houston to Avenue of the Americas.

- **2** or **3** southbound to 14th Street. Switch to **1** or **9** southbound to Houston Street. Walk east on Houston to Avenue of the Americas.

- **A, B, C, D, E** or **F** southbound to West 4th Street. Walk south on Avenue of the Americas to Houston Street.

BUSES

- **M5** southbound on Riverside Drive, then Broadway, then Fifth Avenue, then Broadway, then westbound on Houston Street, to Avenue of the Americas.

- **M6** southbound on Seventh Avenue, then Broadway, then westbound on Houston Street, to Avenue of the Americas.

- **M10** southbound on Central Park West, then Seventh Avenue, then Seventh Avenue South, to Houston Street. Walk east on Houston to Avenue of the Americas.

FROM THE SOUTH
Subways

- **1** or **9** northbound to Houston Street. Walk east on Houston to Avenue of the Americas.

- **2** or **3** northbound to Chambers Street. Switch to **1** or **9** northbound to Houston Street. Walk east on Houston to Avenue of the Americas.

- **A, C** or **E** northbound to West 4th Street. Walk south on Avenue of the Americas to Houston Street.

Buses

- **M6** northbound on Church Street, then Avenue of the Americas, to Houston Street.

- **M10** northbound on West Street, then Hudson Street, to Houston Street. Walk east on Houston to Avenue of the Americas.

FROM THE EAST
Subways

- **B, D** or **F** westbound to West 4th Street. Walk south on Avenue of the Americas to Houston Street.

Buses

- **M21** southbound on Avenue C, then westbound on Houston Street, to Avenue of the Americas.

FROM THE WEST
Buses

- **M21** eastbound on Spring Street, then northbound on Avenue of the Americas, to Houston Street.

At the intersection of Avenue of the Americas and West Houston Street, head west on Houston. The road is relatively narrow, compared to the large eight-lane thoroughfare that is Houston on the east side of Avenue of the Americas. Walk the short distance until you are in front of 195 West Houston Street.

1. 195 West Houston Street. Gilda's Club. For awhile, you couldn't go to the movies without seeing a short film requesting donations to help build this place. Named after the gifted comedienne and actress, Gilda Radner, who died of cancer in 1989, Gilda's Club is a testament to some of the positive aspects of celebrity. Though Gilda is sorely missed, her memory lives on in this center and in the work it does for people stricken with the horrible disease.

Head east until you get back to where you started. Cross Avenue of the Americas and continue east one more block. Turn right on MacDougal Street. Walk south on MacDougal until you reach 38 MacDougal.

2. 38 MacDougal Street. Restaurant Provence. Billed as one of the most romantic restaurants in a city filled with romantic restaurants, Provence is often the place where "guys" pop the

question to their "dolls." In *Crossing Delancey*, however, it is where author Anton Maes (Jeroen Krabbe) took Isabel (Amy Irving), who had a crush on him, for lunch on a first date.

—·—

Continue South on MacDougal and make a left on Prince Street. Stop when you are across from Raoul's.

3. 180 Prince Street. Raoul's Restaurant Francais. Another SoHo favorite, this was the location of the restaurant owned by a different Anton (Tcheky Karyo), the man who stole the heart of Linda (Kelly Preston), the girlfriend of Sam, the Milky Way Man (Matthew Broderick), in *Addicted to Love*. Sam got himself a job as a dishwasher in the restaurant, working for his nemesis, and exacted his revenge, with the help of Maggie (Meg Ryan), the woman spurned by Anton.

—·—

Head slightly east (the same direction you've been heading), until you are across from 172 Prince Street.

4. 172 Prince Street. This seemingly obscure doorway leads to the apartment where Savannah Wingo (Melinda Dillon), the sister of Tom Wingo (Nick Nolte), in *The Prince of Tides*, lived. After Savannah attempted suicide, Tom came to New York and lived in Savannah's apartment, hoping to find out what led his sister to such a desperate act. He did.

—·—

Continue east to 160 Prince Street.

5. 160 Prince Street. Vesuvio Bakery. In that same film, *The Prince of Tides*, Tom Wingo fell into a New York routine, going jogging in the mornings and stopping in here to get some fresh bread.

—·—

Turn back and head west on Prince Street and turn left on Thompson Street. Head south on Thompson until you reach the playground on the right, just before Spring Street.

6. Thompson Street. North of Spring. Handball Court. Frankie (Nick Scotti) caught his girlfriend having sex with his brother, and decided it was time to make a change. He answered an ad for an apartment, and moved in with a "guy with money." At least, that's what he thought "GWM" stood for in the ad, in *Kiss Me, Guido*. He ultimately learned that it meant "gay white male," but by that time, he had nowhere else to live. One afternoon, Frankie and his friend from the Bronx, Joey Chips (Dominick Lombardozzi), played handball on these courts.

One of the few locations I am not 100% sure of, this handball court was also, I believe, used in *Big*. Threatened by the rapid rise of young newcomer Josh Baskin (Tom Hanks), toy company executive Paul (John Heard) challenged Josh to a game of paddleball on these courts. Josh soon learned that in paddleball, as in life, not everyone plays by the rules.

———

Continue south on Thompson and cross Spring Street. Stop at the blue door on the right hand side of the street, at 75 Thompson (the door to the left of 79–81).

7. 75 Thompson Street. After Eliza (Hope Davis) found a love poem among her husband's belongings, she and her entire family packed into their station wagon and drove to New York, to find out what secret her husband, Louis (Stanley Tucci), may have been keeping from her, in *The Daytrippers*. The family staked out this building and, sure enough, watched Louis emerge from behind the blue door with a woman.

Walk back to Spring Street and make a right. Head east five blocks on Spring until you reach Broadway (that's beyond West Broadway). Turn left on Broadway and head north until Prince Street. Look directly across Broadway.

8. 560 Broadway (at Prince Street). Dean & Deluca. While Sam (Matthew Broderick) divided his nights between his two apartments (one he shared with sloppy roommates and one he had by himself, for two nights a week), he spent his days working behind the cheese counter here, in

The Night We Never Met. Little did he know that the woman interested in buying special caviar for a very special occasion shared that apartment with him, and had special plans for the caviar.

Cross Broadway and walk east. Turn left on

Lafayette. Continue north until you reach the massive building on the right, the Puck Building, just south of Houston Street.

9. 295 Lafayette Street. The Puck Building.

Having finally figured out the serial killer's *modus operandi*, fireman-turned-sleuth Nick (Kevin Kline) set out to snare the killer before he struck again inside this building. And with the help of Bernadette (Mary Elizabeth Mastrantonio), who also happened to be the daughter of the Mayor,

in *The January Man*, Nick set out to rid the city of this menace.

———◆·◆———

Turn back south on Lafayette and stop at the alley, just past the south end of the Puck Building.

10. Jersey Street Alleyway. Off Lafayette.

Not the best location to be sure, but this is where falafel vendor Mustafa (Omar Townsend) stood, day after day, trying his best. He had very few customers, but one of them was the very sexy and very persistent Mary (Parker Posey), in *Party Girl*.

———◆·◆———

Continue south on Lafayette and make a left on Prince Street. Walk east one block and turn left at Mulberry Street. Walk north until you reach the red brick wall, just north of the church, on the right.

11. Mulberry Street (between Prince and Jersey Streets). Door in Brick Wall. After Johnny (Robert DeNiro), who was a little out of control, shot his gun from a rooftop, he and Char-

lie (Harvey Keitel) hid out in the cemetery behind this door, in *Mean Streets*.

Years later, Frankie and his friend Joey watched in horror as two guys kissed right in front of this door. A common occurrence in many parts of Manhattan, such a sight was apparently unusual for two guys who worked in a pizzeria in the Bronx, in *Kiss Me, Guido*.

Return to Prince and make a right. Head west on Prince (you will cross both Lafayette and Broadway), and make a left on Mercer Street. Stop when you are in front of 112 Mercer.

12. 112 Mercer Street. A few floors up in this loft building Sam Wheat (Patrick Swayze) and Molly Jensen (Demi Moore) lived together, in *Ghost*. Unlike many New York locations, where only the exteriors of the buildings are used, the scenes that took place in their home were actually filmed inside the building.

Continue south on Mercer until you get to Spring Street.

Tour 12

13. Spring Street and Mercer Street. Intersection. After a lunch that could only be described as awkward, Max (Wesley Snipes), Mimi (Ming-Na Wen), Karen (Nastassja Kinski) and Vernon (Kyle MacLachlan) stood at this intersec-

tion. In *One Night Stand*, we learned that much had happened to these two couples, and that a one night stand was not always just a one night stand.

Continue south on Mercer until you reach Grand Street. Turn right on Grand and head west until you get to Avenue of the Americas. Turn right on Avenue of the Americas and walk north to 110 Avenue of the Americas, at Watt Street (Lupe's East L.A. Kitchen).

14. 110 Avenue of the Americas (at Watt Street). Northeast Corner. Lupe's East L.A. Kitchen. Poor Charlie Driggs (Jeff Daniels). Seemingly content with his none-too-exciting existence, he came here for a peaceful lunch. After lunch, he met Lulu (Melanie Griffith), who offered to drive him back to his office. She kidnapped him instead and took Charlie for the ride of his life, in *Something Wild*.

Head back south on Avenue of the Americas.

Stop at the corner of Avenue of the Americas and Grand Street.

15. Avenue of the Americas and Grand Street. Moondance Diner. Although Monica Geller (Courtney Cox), one of television's "Friends," wants nothing more than to be a chef, for a short while she had to settle for working here as a waitress. To make matters worse, she was forced to wear a padded bra and tacky blond wig while serving her customers.

Continue south on Avenue of the Americas to Canal Street. Cross to the far side of Canal Street (where it merges with Laight Street), then turn right on Laight and head west to Varick Street. You are now in TriBeCa. Make a left on Varick and head south to North Moore Street.

16. Varick and North Moore Streets. Hook & Ladder 8. If you can picture the Ghostbusters logo over the entranceway, you've figured this one out. Thanks to the generosity of Ray (Dan

Aykroyd), and the banks who let him take out multiple mortgages on his family's home, Ray, Peter (Bill Murray) and Egon (Harold Ramis)

moved their operation into this building, in *Ghostbusters,* after their funding at Columbia University (see **Walking Tour 3: The (Upper) Upper West Side**) was cut.

Turn right at the firehouse and cross Varick. Head west on North Moore Street and make a left on Greenwich Street (tall buildings will loom across the street). Head south on Greenwich until you come to Harrison Street.

17. Harrison and Greenwich Streets. Running into an "ex" is always an awkward moment. It is even worse when the ex is with someone new and you are not. In *Husbands and Wives,* Jack (Sydney Pollack) and Sally (Judy Davis) had separated and Sally was walking with friends Gabe (Woody Allen) and Judy (Mia Farrow), when they ran into Jack and his new girlfriend, Sam (Lysette Anthony), at this corner.

You have now reached the end of **Walking Tour 12: SoHo and TriBeCa**. If you can see the twin towers of the World Trade Center just a short distance to the south, then you are within walking distance of the beginning of **Walking Tour 13: Downtown and Financial District**. You may not get a better chance than this.

DOWNTOWN AND FINANCIAL DISTRICT

Walking Tour 13

DOWNTOWN AND FINANCIAL DISTRICT

Still considered to be the financial capital of the world, downtown Manhattan, encompassing the New York Stock Exchange and the headquarters of major banks and brokerage houses, is also a favorite among filmmakers.

Walking Tour 13: Downtown and Financial District, begins, fittingly enough, at the World Trade Center. If you choose to get to the starting point by public transportation, you may use any of the following subway or bus lines (although the following list is by no means exhaustive):

FROM THE NORTH

SUBWAYS

- **1, 9, N** or **R** southbound to Cortlandt Street/World Trade Center.

- **2** or **3** southbound to Chambers Street. Switch to **1** or **9** southbound to Cortlandt Street/World Trade Center.

- **E** southbound to World Trade Center.

BUSES

- **M6** southbound on Seventh Avenue, then Broadway, to Vesey Street. Walk west on Vesey to World Trade Center.

- **M10** southbound on Central Park West, then Seventh Avenue, then Seventh Avenue South, then Varick Street, then West Broadway, to World Trade Center.

FROM THE SOUTH
SUBWAYS
- **1, 9, N** or **R** northbound to Cortlandt Street/World Trade Center.

BUSES
- **M6** northbound on Trinity Place to World Trade Center.

FROM THE EAST
BUSES
- **M9** westbound on East Broadway, then Park Row, then Barclay Street, to World Trade Center.
- **M22** westbound on Madison Street [not Madison Avenue], then Chambers Street, to World Trade Center.

FROM THE WEST
BUSES
- **M9** northbound on South End Avenue [Battery Park City], to World Trade Center.
- **M22** eastbound on Vesey Street to World Trade Center.

No longer the tallest buildings in the world, thanks to structures in Chicago and Malaysia, the World Trade Center's Twin Towers are nevertheless as impressive in size as any other buildings anywhere.

If you are currently standing in the Concourse and would like to take a quick detour to the World Financial Center and Location 1, now is a good time to do it. [Note: taking this detour may cause the Walking Tour to exceed two hours in duration, but only slightly.] Follow the signs for the World Financial Center; the route is clearly marked. If you prefer not to take this detour, skip to the directions for Location 2.

Walk through the Concourse (an enormous, enclosed shopping mall) and follow the signs for the World Financial Center. You will have to enter

244

One World Trade Center in order to reach the overpass that will take you to the World Financial Center. Once inside One World Trade Center, walk toward the right and turn right past the Visitor's Desk.[5] Go up the escalator and cross West Street in the enclosed overpass. You will emerge, through revolving doors, at the top of the Winter Garden in the World Financial Center.

1. Winter Garden. World Financial Center. His book having become a bestseller, writer Peter Fallow (Bruce Willis), in a perpetual drunken state, was escorted to a waiting crowd to celebrate his success. The movie is *The Bonfire of the Vanities*, and the crowd filled the Winter Garden below. As he stood before the cheering mass, Peter Fallow began to relate the incredible story that got him to where he was on that day.

Retrace your steps out of the Winter Garden, back across West Street through the North Bridge overpass, down the escalators and left through One World Trade Center until you reach the Concourse. The next step is to find your way out of the World Trade Center Concourse. If possible, exit toward Liberty Street. Do not enter Two World Trade Center.

As you exit from beneath the Towers, turn left and walk toward Church Street. At the intersection of Church and Liberty, look up high, toward the top of the Twin Towers.

2. World Trade Center. Twin Towers. Although most of the movie took place in Philadelphia, Billy Ray Valentine (Eddie Murphy) and Louis Winthorp (Dan Aykroyd) had to come to New York to exact their revenge on the Duke Brothers (Ralph Bellamy and Don Ameche), in *Trading Places*. After taking the train

---

[5] If you enter from West Street, go toward the left and turn left before the Visitor's Desk.

to New York, the two victims of the Dukes' little nature-vs.-nurture bet emerged from a car at the foot of the Twin Towers, and saw the impressive view before you now.

The headquarters of the CIA, where Deputy Director Higgins (Cliff Robertson) worked and was causing Joe Turner (Robert Redford) a really bad time, were also located in one of these towers, in *Three Days of the Condor.*

Walk east on Liberty Street (away from the Twin Towers) until you get to Broadway. Turn right and walk south until you reach the south side of Wall Street. Turn left on Wall Street and walk east to the intersection of Wall and Broad Streets. Across the street, to the left, you will see the Federal Building.

3. Wall Street and Broad Street. The Federal Building. As you gaze at the statue of George Washington, you may remember the scene in *Ghost* where a reluctant Oda Mae Brown (Whoopi Goldberg), at the insistence of Sam

Wheat (Patrick Swayze), gave away to the shocked nuns from the Saint Joseph's Shelter for the Homeless the $4,000,000 that she had withdrawn from the murderous Carl's (Tony Goldwyn) bank account. The transaction took place at the base of the statue.

On a less peaceful day, New York's Mayor Ebert (Michael Lerner) was giving a speech in front of this building. The speech ended abruptly when the beast known as Godzilla stepped ashore in lower Manhattan, in *Godzilla*.

Continue east on Wall Street until you pass William Street. Just past William, walk to the top of the stairs on the left, leading down to the subway.

4. Wall Street and William Street. Subway Entrance. It was a festive night, and Charlie (Woody Harrelson) had had too much to drink. Or had he? He stumbled down Wall Street and made his way gingerly down this staircase. As it turned out, Charlie was an undercover cop for the transit police Decoy Squad and his behavior was all in a night's work, in *Money Train*.

Note the big door, just east of the subway stairs.

5. 48 Wall Street. Things didn't go according to plan and Steven Taylor (Michael Douglas) had to give $400,000 to David Shaw (Viggo Mortensen) to keep him from telling the authorities what the two had planned, in *A Perfect Murder*. Steven came to a bank at this location to withdraw the money from his account.

Return to William Street and turn left. Walk one block to Exchange Place.

6. Exchange Place and William Street. Southeast Corner. After setting out on her own, Laurel Ayres (Whoopi Goldberg) had to have an office, which she found here, along with her loyal assistant Sally (Dianne Wiest), in *The Associate*.

Continue south on William Street one block, until you reach Beaver Street.

7. 56 Beaver Street. Delmonico's. Earlier in *The Associate*, Laurel knew that something was wrong when Sally pointed out Laurel's colleague, Frank (Tim Daly), coming out of Delmonico's after a lunch with their boss, Walter (George Martin)—a lunch that Laurel should have been part of.

Head back to Exchange Place and turn left. Walk west until you reach Broad Street. Turn left on Broad until you are across from 40 Broad Street.

8. 40 Broad Street. This building, which sits just south and west of the subway station entrance with its distinctive red-and-white globes on the light poles, is where Lawrence Garfield (Danny DeVito) worked as a takeover king, in *Other Peoples' Money*. In the movie, he is seen leaving his limousine and entering the office building.

Again return to Exchange Place and make a left, now walking the short distance to Broadway. Cross to the far side of Broadway, turn right and walk north until you are in front of 71 Broadway.

9. 71 Broadway. Editor Henry Hackett (Michael Keaton) had it pretty rough. His wife Martha

(Marisa Tomei) was pregnant and feeling scared and vulnerable, and Henry was facing a deadline to put his paper to bed. The offices for that paper, *The New York Sun*, were located in this building, in *The Paper*.

Head back the other way, going south on Broadway. Continue until you are across from the statue of the bull that adorns the island of land just as Broadway splits. Look across Broadway, to number 26.

10. 26 Broadway. Against his better judgment, Bud Fox (Charlie Sheen) agreed to do some dirty work for Gordon Gecko (Oscar-winner Michael Douglas), in *Wall Street*. Bud had to trail British financier Larry Wildman (Terrence Stamp) to find out what he was doing in town. Bud hopped his motorcycle, tracked Larry's Rolls Royce downtown and followed him into this building at 26 Broadway. Bud even managed to force his way onto the same elevator as Larry and his entourage.

In another film, Monty Brewster (Richard Pryor) had just seen the $30,000,000 he had inherited in *Brewster's Millions*. It was piled high in a vault at The First Bank of Manhattan, which I am pretty sure was also located in this building.

Continue south on Broadway until you get to the circular plaza at the end of Broadway, with the large museum building (identified as "U.S. Custom House" near the top) on your left. Walk to the museum and turn to face the plaza in front.

11. 1 Bowling Green. Museum. It had been quite a year for cop-turned-lawyer Sean Casey (Andy Garcia). After his father was shot in a drug bust, Sean was selected as the Assistant District Attorney who would prosecute the defendant. And, before long, his boss the District Attorney,

Morgie (Ron Liebman), was felled by a stroke, and Sean was elected to succeed him. During a restless evening Sean, knowing that police corruption had hit particularly close to home, wandered the streets of lower Manhattan, finally ending up at this building, trying to decide what to do, in *Night Falls on Manhattan*.

Convinced he was the target of a giant conspiracy in which everyone was out to get him, cabdriver Jerry Fletcher (Mel Gibson) made a habit of barging in on Justice Department employee Alice Sutton (Julia Roberts), in *Conspiracy Theory*. In the movie, the Justice Department offices were located in this building.

Turn left and cross over to the park side of the intersection. Walk west on the street just north of Battery Park (Battery Place) until you are across from the windowless building just west of Greenwich Street.

12. Battery Place (between Greenwich and Washington Streets). Administration Building. Beneath this seemingly innocuous building the highly secretive organization that tracked and fought alien invaders was located, in *Men in Black*. In several scenes, we see Kay (Tommy Lee Jones) and Jay (Will Smith) walk into this building.

Walk into Battery Park and turn to the right after you pass the Hope Garden. You should be heading in the direction of Castle Clinton National Monument. As you near the Monument, walk to the left of Castle Clinton and around it. Take one of the paths and head toward the water. As you approach Admiral Dewey Promenade, the Statue of Liberty should be plainly in view.

13. Battery Park. Admiral Dewey Promenade. Statue of Liberty in View.

College freshman Clark Kellogg (Matthew Broderick) had gotten himself in a hell of a mess, one involving agents of the federal government, a rare but apparently tasty komodo dragon, and a mysterious man who bore more than a striking resemblance to Don Corleone from a certain film about the Mafia. It was no coincidence, of course, that the man was played by Marlon Brando, in full Corleone regalia. This movie is *The Freshman*, and in it Clark stood at the railing in front of you, staring at the Statue of Liberty and contemplating his next move.

Adrift and alone in New York, Kevin McAllister (Macaulay Culkin) rose to the occasion and took himself on a whirlwind tour of Manhattan, in *Home Alone 2: Lost in New York*. In one scene, Kevin stood along the same railing as Clark Kellogg, and admired the Statue of Liberty through one of the viewing machines just above the promenade.

If Clark and Kevin had really been lucky, they might have seen a mermaid (Daryl Hannah) emerge from the waters of the Hudson River, clamber up onto Liberty Island and approach the Statue of Liberty, much to the shock and delight of onlookers, in *Splash*.

———————

Continue walking toward the railing. As you get to the Admiral Dewey Promenade along the river, turn left and walk along the promenade.

14. Battery Park. Admiral Dewey Promenade. Bored with her life as a housewife, Roberta (Rosanna Arquette) sought excitement,

and found it in the life of Susan (Madonna), in *Desperately Seeking Susan*. In one scene, Roberta had an encounter along this promenade with someone who was searching for Susan.

———•◆•———

Turn toward Castle Clinton and find a bench near the water, as close to Castle Clinton as possible.

15. Bench on Promenade. Near Castle Clinton. Veteran operative Kay and potential newcomer Jay sat on one of these benches, in *Men in Black* while Kay laid out for Jay just what his job in the alien-monitoring organization would entail. Required to sever all his human ties, Jay was unsure of what to do, and he spent the rest of the day and night sitting on the same bench right here, weighing his decision.

———•◆•———

Continue walking south along the Admiral Dewey Promenade and make a left up the steps past the United States Navy Monument. Walk past the statue of the eagle, turn right and follow the path around, keeping the fenced-in grassy area on your left. As you near the exit to the park, bear right (do not walk toward the building called "17 State"). Exit the park, cross State Street and cross to Peter Minuit Plaza, across from the Staten Island Ferry Terminal.

16. Staten Island Ferry Terminal. Hoping to improve her lot in life, secretary Tess McGill (Melanie Griffith), in *Working Girl*, took the

Staten Island Ferry each day, to and from her home in Staten Island. This terminal is where she disembarked in Manhattan.

Turn from the Terminal building and head east (away from Battery Park). You should be on Water Street. Continue walking east (which gradually turns into a northern direction) until you reach the Vietnam Memorial Plaza.

17. Vietnam Memorial. Water Street and Coenties Slip. Having learned that it could take six weeks to find out where the Zoltar machine that had granted his "wish" had gone, Josh Baskin (Tom Hanks) and friend Billy Kopecki (Jared Rushton) spent a few minutes hanging out in this plaza, in *Big*.

Continue in the same direction along Water

Street until you reach Pine Street. Turn right on Pine and walk through the plaza to Front Street. Make a left on Front and walk to Maiden Lane.

18. 180 Maiden Lane (at Front Street). Until she went out on her own, Laurel Ayres worked for Manchester, in this building, in *The Associate*.

———◆·◆———

Head back on Front Street and make a left on Wall Street. Cross South Street (the elevated F.D.R. Drive should appear above you). Cross under the F.D.R. Drive and walk to the tennis courts.

19. Wall Street Tennis Courts. Wall Street and East River. Having just met as part of a blind date to play tennis with some friends, Alvie Singer (Woody Allen) and Annie Hall (Diane Keaton) emerged from these courts, in *Annie Hall*. Annie offered Alvie a wild ride home in her Volkswagon Beetle.

———◆·◆———

Walk north along the fence by the tennis courts, until you reach the South Street Seaport. The structure directly in front of you, on the east side of the F.D.R. Drive (and South Street), is known as Pier 17. Walk to the right along Pier 17 and circle the building. When you get to the other side, walk to the fence. The Brooklyn Bridge should be in view.

20. Pier 17. The East River. After dating for awhile, Alvie told Annie, in *Annie Hall*, while standing along the railing right here, that she was not only very sexy, but also "polymorphously perverse." Neither she nor we were quite sure what he meant, but they end up together at least for awhile, so it could not have been too bad.

In another film, the railing was gone, but on this same spot, Allen Bauer (Tom Hanks) stood saying farewell to his love, Madison (Daryl Han-

nah), in *Splash*. They realized that she, a fish-out-of-water, could no longer live in his world, and he surely couldn't follow her into hers. And then again, maybe true love does conquer all. Hoping beyond hope, Allen jumped into the cold East River waters after Madison.

Retrace your steps to the other end of Pier 17. Head toward South Street but before you cross, turn and notice the metal staircase leading up to the second-floor restaurant.

21. Pier 17. Staircase. Having just bonded with the sexy Tess McGill at what otherwise would have been a boring corporate event in *Working Girl*, Jack Trainer (Harrison Ford) descended this staircase, anticipating an evening filled with lush rewards. As he reached the bottom of the stairs, with Tess's coat in hand, he noticed the legs of a very drunk Tess sticking out from the backseat of a waiting taxicab.

Even though he would later tell her of their night together that the earth moved and the angels wept, it would be awhile before she would become his working girl and he her working guy.

Before crossing South Street, look down at your feet.

22. South Street and the Seaport. You should

know that you are standing in the very spot where Godzilla first stepped, when he emerged from the East River to create havoc in Manhattan, in *Godzilla*.

———◆·◆———

Walk west, with the South Street Seaport on your right. Make a left on Water Street and walk south until you get to Wall Street Plaza, between Maiden Lane and Pine Street. Stop at the tree closest to the main entrance.

23. Wall Street Plaza (between Maiden Lane and Pine Street). Tree. Imagine you are Bud Fox and had just learned that your idol, Gordon Gecko, had pulled a fast one on you, and was planning to dismantle your father's company (Blue Star Airlines) once he had taken it over,

thanks to your help, in *Wall Street*. Shocked, d i s m a y e d , numb, you left the meeting of lawyers and finance people, walked along Water Street and stopped at this tree, leaning up against it for support. That's what Bud Fox did. Right here.

———◆·◆———

Head back north on Water Street to the north side of Maiden Lane. Make a left on Maiden Lane and cross Water Street. Walk west on Maiden Lane until you reach Gold Street. At Gold, note the building with the castle-like tower in front of you.

24. William and Liberty Streets. Federal Reserve Building. A madman was loose in Manhattan, and had planted enough bombs all over the place to occupy the time of John McClane (Bruce Willis), his colleague Zeus (Samuel L. Jackson) and the rest of the New York police force, in *Die Hard With a Vengeance*. While the cops searched for a bomb in every school, the madman Simon (Jeremy Irons) led his team into the Federal Reserve Building intent on removing the city's gold supply. Some went in through the front entrance, others drove trucks along the side of the building, through a hole created by the bomb detonated on a number 3 subway train.

Continue walking in the same direction on Maiden Lane until you reach Nassau Street. Turn right on Nassau and walk north until you reach the end. Pace University should be in front of you, toward the right. You might notice the large building in the distance, on the north side of the Brooklyn Bridge. Hold that image for a few minutes.

Turn left and walk to Park Row. Cross Park Row and walk north along City Hall Park, until City Hall comes clearly into view.

25. City Hall. Park Row. Office of the real Mayor of New York as well as various fictional mayors in the movies, this is where Mayor John Pappas (Al Pacino) worked in *City Hall;* where Jack Taylor (George Clooney) confronted the Mayor known as Sidney (Sid Armus), about corruption in the sanitation industry, in *One Fine Day;* where the Ghostbusters convinced the Mayor known as Lenny (David Margulies), in *Ghostbusters,* that the days of fire and brimstone had fallen on the city, thanks in no small part to the interference of low-level public servant Mr. Peck (William Atherton); and where Mayor Flynn (Rod Steiger) struggled to protect both his daughter Bernadette (Mary Elizabeth Mastrantonio) and his city from the reign of terror of a serial killer, in *The January Man*.

———◆—◆———

Walk north past City Hall until you reach the corner of Chambers Street and Center Street. Turn to the right and get a close-up of that building you first noticed from Nassau Street. Cross Chambers Street (following the crossing signs) and then cross Centre Street. Walk toward the Municipal Building.

26. 1 Centre Street. The Municipal Building.

In a pivotal scene in *Ghostbusters*, after the ghost-busting guys convinced the Mayor that the demons must be stopped, the army was seen mobilizing from beneath the arch of this building.

After his source, Manny Feldstein (Joe Grifasi), in *One Fine Day*, backed away from his corruption story, Jack Taylor spotted him outside this building, followed him inside and chased him to the roof.

In yet another movie where corruption abounded, Deputy Mayor Kevin Calhoun (John Cusack) and Abe (David Paymer) paid a visit to Larry Schwartz (Richard Schiff) of the Department of Probation, located in this building, in *City Hall*.

———◆—◆———

Turn toward the right and walk toward the archway. Centre Street should be on your right. Just through the archway, there should be a bench on the right hand side. If not, imagine that it's there anyway. It was in the movie.

27. 1 Centre Street. Municipal Building. Bench under Archway.

Having "lost" a case that his office had considered not capable of being lost, soon-to-be former Assistant District Attorney Michael (Brad Pitt) sat on a bench right here with life-long friend Shakes (Jason Patric), contemplating his next move, in *Sleepers*.

Continue under the archway. Pause at the top of the stairs leading to the subway.

28. 1 Centre Street. Subway Station Stairs. Would-be muggers at this location pulled a knife on Mick Dundee (Paul Hogan) and his girlfriend Sue (Linda Kozlowski), in *"Crocodile" Dundee*. Not impressed by the puny knife sported by the

muggers, Dundee declared in his inimitable Australian accent, "That's not a knife," and thereupon pulled out his own much larger weapon and displayed it for all to see, "*that's* a knife."

If you stand at the top of the stairs long enough, you may see undercover transit cops Charlie and John (Wesley Snipes) pass you as they descend these stairs. They did just that, in *Money Train,* after being chewed out by their boss, Chief Patterson (Robert Blake).

Walk around behind the Municipal Building, away from the Brooklyn Bridge. But get a good look at the bridge if you can.

29. Brooklyn Bridge. New York was under siege from terrorists, who had already blown up a bus, a theatre and a government office building. After the president gave the order, the army was mobilized and, led by General Bill Devereaux (Bruce Willis), lumbered over the Brooklyn Bridge and set up camp, in *The Siege.*

Continue away from the Bridge until you are standing in the plaza leading to One Police Plaza. The red sculpture should be on your left.

30. One Police Plaza. The movie was *Cop Land*, and mild-mannered but righteous cop Freddy Heflin (Sylvester Stallone), having stood up to the rogue cops for the first time in his career, delivered cop-in-hiding Murray (Michael Rapaport) into the waiting hands of Internal Affairs detective Moe Tilden (Robert DeNiro), right in front of One Police Plaza.

Turn left and, with One Police Plaza to your right and the Municipal Building to your left, walk through the plaza, with the Catholic Church of St. Andrew across the way, until you get back to Centre Street.

31. Municipal Building Plaza. In *The Devil's Advocate*, senior partner of all senior partners John Milton (Al Pacino) walked alongside young protégé Kevin Lomax (Keanu Reeves) in this plaza. As they crossed the street, Milton offered to take Kevin off the big murder case he had been work-

ing on so he could tend to his ailing wife, but Kevin declined.

This plaza must remind filmmakers of the devil, because it was used in another recent devil movie. In *The Devil's Own*, after escaping from the back of a police car and shooting officer Eddie Diaz (Ruben Blades), Rory/Frankie (Brad Pitt) ran through this same plaza, with officer Tom O'Meara (Harrison Ford) in hot pursuit.

Turn right and head north on Centre Street. You should immediately see the impressive federal courthouse, at 40 Centre Street, and the state court building, one block beyond that, at 60 Centre Street. Continue until you reach 60 Centre Street.

32. 60 Centre Street. New York Supreme Court Building. The year was 1947, and Santa Claus was on trial in New York City. Only a miracle could save him, and that miracle was delivered, thanks to the love and faith of Susan (a very young Natalie Wood), the belief of Doris (Maureen O'Hara), the legal skills of Fred (John Payne) and some misdirected mail, courtesy of the United States Post Office. The verdict: the man on trial, Kris Kringle (Edmund Gwenn), must be Santa Claus. The movie: *Miracle on 34th Street,* and the courtroom scenes took place in this building.

Little did people watching the trial of Kris Kringle know that, years later, more sinister happenings would occur on the front steps of the courthouse. In *The Godfather*, Michael Corleone (Al Pacino) decided to exact his revenge on the heads of the other New York families before orchestrating his own family's move to Nevada. In a classic scene, while his godson was being baptized, Michael knew that at the same time five men were being assassinated by his people. The head of one of those families was gunned down by a man impersonating a police officer, as he walked down the steps of this building.

Luckily, Pacino did not meet a similar fate years later when he himself descended these same steps. Justice having supposedly been served, Carlito Grigante (Al Pacino), whose conviction had just been overturned after he had spent five years in prison, exulted in his freedom as he walked down the steps with his attorney, Dave Kleinfeld (Sean Penn), in *Carlito's Way*.

In the final scene of *Wall Street*, after his arrest for insider trading, Bud Fox was dropped off in front of the courthouse and was seen walking up the long steps to the front door to face the music.

Recently-teamed legal eagles Tom Logan (Robert Redford) and Laura J. Kelly (Debra

Winger) defended Chelsea Dierdon (Daryl Hannah) in her trial for murder in this building, in *Legal Eagles*.

———•◆•———

Continue north on Centre Street. Two buildings up on the right (just north of Hogan Place) will be the imposing Criminal Court House, located at 100 Centre Street.

33. 100 Centre Street. Criminal Court. Two out-of-town businessmen were found shot to death in a car and two young men were arrested for the crime. While crowds of reporters waited outside this building for the men to emerge, Michael Keaton's assistant Robin (Amelia Campbell) struggled to get a good photo for their story, in *The Paper*.

Still trying to get to the bottom of the conspiracy, Jerry followed a familiar-looking man into this building. He noticed "Dept. of Commerce" on the directory in the lobby, which confirmed his belief that "spooks" (*i.e.*, CIA) operated from somewhere within the building, in *Conspiracy Theory*.

———•◆•———

Cross Centre Street and head south, back toward City Hall. At Worth Street, turn to the right. You will see a very tall, modern-looking building directly across from the Supreme Court building, on Federal Plaza, at the intersection of Lafayette and Worth Streets.

34. 26 Federal Plaza. Their marriage was a sham, just a way for Georges (Gerard Depardieu) to get a green card so he could stay in the United States. But the Immigration Service caught up with Georges and Bronte (Andie MacDowell), in *Green Card* and made them take a test to determine if they were really married. After the test, they walked out of this building to ponder their fate.

You have now reached the end of the final Walking Tour, **Walking Tour 13: Downtown and Financial District**. I hope you enjoyed it. This is a great city with lots of things to do. If you haven't yet taken all of the other tours, how about another Walking Tour?

Movie Index

About the Author

huck Katz grew up in a family of six on New York's Long Island, in Island Park, a town that did not find its way into too many movies. He attended Union College in upstate New York (where scenes from *The Way We Were* had been filmed) and Fordham Law School (one block from Location 34 of **Walking Tour 2: The (Lower) Upper West Side**).

Mr. Katz practiced law in New York City from 1984–1998, the last 12 years specializing in Public Finance. An amateur photographer (all photographs appearing in the book that are not movie stills have been taken by the author), Mr. Katz has been profiled in the ABA Journal and his song parodies have appeared in industry publications.

In addition to *Manhattan on Film,* Mr. Katz has written a novel, two screenplays, and ten television scripts.

Mr. Katz has lived on Hollywood's Fabled Front Lot since 1981.